HERSHEY'S®

Favorite Recipes

Publications International, Ltd.

Pictured on the front cover: Creme de Cacao Torte *(page 146)*.
Pictured on the back cover *(top to bottom)*: Chocolate Macaroon Bars *(page 36)*, Easy Chocolate Mousse-Filled Tulip Cups *(page 148)*, and Crispy Chocolate Ice Cream Mud Pie *(page 152)*.

ISBN 13: 978-1-4508-5952-3
ISBN 10: 1-4508-5952-6

Library of Congress Control Number: 2012955146

Manufactured in China.

8 7 6 5 4 3 2 1

Microwave Cooking: Microwave ovens vary in wattage. Use the cooking times as guidelines and check for doneness before adding more time.

Table of Contents

Brownies,
Bars
& Cookies

English Toffee Bars

Makes 24 to 36 bars

2 cups all-purpose flour

1 cup packed light brown sugar

1/2 cup (1 stick) cold butter

1 cup pecan halves

TOFFEE TOPPING (recipe follows)

1 cup HERSHEY'S Milk Chocolate Chips

1. Heat oven to 350°F.

2. Combine flour and brown sugar in large bowl. With pastry blender or fork, cut in butter until fine crumbs form (a few large crumbs may remain). Press mixture onto bottom of ungreased 13×9×2-inch baking pan. Sprinkle pecans over crust.

Prepare TOFFEE TOPPING; drizzle evenly over pecans and crust.

3. Bake 20 to 22 minutes or until topping is bubbly and golden; remove from oven. Immediately sprinkle milk chocolate chips evenly over top; press gently onto surface. Cool completely in pan on wire rack. Cut into bars.

Toffee Topping: Combine 2/3 cup butter and 1/3 cup packed light brown sugar in small saucepan; cook over medium heat, stirring constantly, until mixture comes to a boil. Continue boiling, stirring constantly, 30 seconds. Use immediately.

Chocolate Fudge Pecan Pie Bars

Makes about 36 bars

2²/₃ **cups all-purpose flour**

1¹/₄ **cups packed light brown sugar, divided**

1 **cup (2 sticks) cold butter or margarine**

4 **eggs**

1 **cup light corn syrup**

1 **package (4 ounces) HERSHEY'S Unsweetened Chocolate Baking Bar, unwrapped and melted**

2 **teaspoons vanilla extract**

¹/₂ **teaspoon salt**

2 **cups coarsely chopped pecans**

1. Heat oven to 350°F. Grease 15¹/₂×10¹/₂×1-inch jelly-roll pan.

2. Stir together flour and ¹/₄ cup brown sugar in large bowl. With pastry blender, cut in butter until mixture resembles coarse crumbs; press onto bottom and about ¹/₂ inch up sides of prepared pan.

3. Bake 10 to 15 minutes or until set. Remove from oven. With back of spoon, lightly press crust into corners and against sides of pan.

4. Beat eggs, corn syrup, remaining 1 cup brown sugar, melted chocolate, vanilla and salt; stir in pecans. Pour mixture evenly over warm crust. Return to oven.

5. Bake 25 to 30 minutes or until chocolate filling is set. Cool completely in pan on wire rack. Cut into bars.

Lemon Coconut Pixies

¹/₄ cup (¹/₂ stick) butter or margarine, softened

1 cup granulated sugar

2 eggs

1¹/₂ teaspoons freshly grated lemon peel

1¹/₂ cups all-purpose flour

2 teaspoons baking powder

¹/₄ teaspoon salt

1 cup MOUNDS Sweetened Coconut Flakes

Powdered sugar

1. Heat oven to 300°F.

2. Beat butter, granulated sugar, eggs and lemon peel in large bowl until well blended. Stir together flour, baking powder and salt; gradually add to lemon mixture, beating until blended. Stir in coconut. Cover; refrigerate dough about 1 hour or until firm enough to handle. Shape into 1-inch balls; roll in powdered sugar. Place 2 inches apart on ungreased cookie sheet.

3. Bake 15 to 18 minutes or until edges are set. Immediately remove from cookie sheet to wire rack. Cool completely. Store in tightly covered container in cool, dry place.

Peanut Butter Glazed Chocolate Bars

³/₄ cup (1¹/₂ sticks) butter or margarine

¹/₂ cup HERSHEY'S Cocoa

1¹/₂ cups sugar

1¹/₂ teaspoons vanilla extract

3 eggs

1¹/₄ cups all-purpose flour

¹/₄ teaspoon baking powder

　　PEANUT BUTTER FILLING
　　AND GLAZE (recipe
　　follows)

　　CHOCOLATE DRIZZLE
　　(recipe follows)

1. Heat oven to 350°F. Line 15¹/₂×10¹/₂×1-inch jelly-roll pan with foil; grease foil.

2. Melt butter in medium saucepan over low heat. Add cocoa; stir constantly until smooth. Remove from heat; stir in sugar and vanilla. Beat in eggs, one at a time, until well combined. Stir in flour and baking powder. Spread batter evenly in prepared pan.

3. Bake 14 to 16 minutes or until top springs back when touched lightly in center. Remove from oven; cool 2 minutes. Invert onto wire rack. Peel off foil; turn right side up on wire rack to cool completely.

4. Prepare PEANUT BUTTER FILLING AND GLAZE. Cut brownie in half; spread half of glaze evenly on one half. Top with second half; spread with remaining glaze. Cool until glaze is set. Prepare CHOCOLATE DRIZZLE; drizzle over glaze. After chocolate is set, cut into bars.

Peanut Butter Filling and Glaze: Combine ¹/₃ cup sugar and ¹/₃ cup water in small saucepan; cook over medium heat to boiling. Remove from heat; immediately add 1²/₃ cups (10-ounce package) REESE'S Peanut Butter Chips. Stir until melted. Cool slightly. Makes about 1¹/₃ cups glaze.

Chocolate Drizzle: Place ¹/₃ cup HERSHEY'S SPECIAL DARK Chocolate Chips or HERSHEY'S Semi-Sweet Chocolate Chips and 1 teaspoon shortening (do not use butter, margarine, spread or oil) in small microwave-safe bowl. Microwave at MEDIUM (50%) 30 seconds to 1 minute or until chips are melted and mixture is smooth when stirred.

Peanut Butter Blossoms

48 **HERSHEY'S KISSES**BRAND **Milk Chocolates**

³/₄ **cup REESE'S Creamy Peanut Butter**

¹/₂ **cup shortening**

¹/₃ **cup granulated sugar**

¹/₃ **cup packed light brown sugar**

1 **egg**

2 **tablespoons milk**

1 **teaspoon vanilla extract**

1¹/₂ **cups all-purpose flour**

1 **teaspoon baking soda**

¹/₂ **teaspoon salt**

   Granulated sugar

1. Heat oven to 375°F. Remove wrappers from chocolates.

2. Beat peanut butter and shortening with electric mixer on medium speed in large bowl until well blended. Add ¹/₃ cup granulated sugar and brown sugar; beat until fluffy. Add egg, milk and vanilla; beat well. Stir together flour, baking soda and salt; gradually beat into peanut butter mixture.

3. Shape dough into 1-inch balls. Roll in additional granulated sugar; place on ungreased cookie sheet.

4. Bake 8 to 10 minutes or until lightly browned. Immediately press a chocolate into center of each cookie; cookies will crack around edges. Remove to wire racks and cool completely.

Brownies, Bars & Cookies

Peanut Butter Fudge Brownie Bars

Makes 24 to 36 bars

1 cup (2 sticks) butter or margarine, melted

1 1/2 cups sugar

2 eggs

1 teaspoon vanilla extract

1 1/4 cups all-purpose flour

2/3 cup HERSHEY'S Cocoa

1/4 cup milk

1 1/4 cups chopped pecans or walnuts, divided

1/2 cup (1 stick) butter or margarine

1 2/3 cups (10-ounce package) REESE'S Peanut Butter Chips

1 can (14 ounces) sweetened condensed milk (not evaporated milk)

1/4 cup HERSHEY'S SPECIAL DARK Chocolate Chips or HERSHEY'S Semi-Sweet Chocolate Chips

1. Heat oven to 350°F. Grease 13×9×2-inch baking pan.

2. Beat melted butter, sugar, eggs and vanilla in large bowl with electric mixer on medium speed until well blended. Add flour, cocoa and milk; beat until blended. Stir in 1 cup nuts. Spread in prepared pan.

3. Bake 25 to 30 minutes or just until edges begin to pull away from sides of pan. Cool completely in pan on wire rack.

4. Melt 1/2 cup butter and peanut butter chips in medium saucepan over low heat, stirring constantly. Add sweetened condensed milk, stirring until smooth; pour over baked layer.

5. Place chocolate chips in small microwave-safe bowl. Microwave at MEDIUM (50%) 45 seconds or just until chips are melted when stirred. Drizzle bars with melted chocolate; sprinkle with remaining 1/4 cup nuts. Refrigerate 1 hour or until firm. Cut into bars. Cover; refrigerate leftover bars.

Mini Brownie Cups

$^1/_4$ cup ($^1/_2$ stick) light margarine

2 egg whites

1 egg

$^3/_4$ cup sugar

$^2/_3$ cup all-purpose flour

$^1/_3$ cup HERSHEY'S Cocoa

$^1/_2$ teaspoon baking powder

$^1/_4$ teaspoon salt

MOCHA GLAZE (recipe follows)

1. Heat oven to 350°F. Line small muffin cups (1$^3/_4$ inches in diameter) with paper bake cups or spray with vegetable cooking spray.

2. Melt margarine in small saucepan over low heat; cool slightly. Beat egg whites and egg in small bowl with electric mixer on medium speed until foamy; gradually add sugar, beating until slightly thickened and light in color. Stir together flour, cocoa, baking powder and salt; gradually add to egg mixture, beating until blended. Gradually add melted margarine, beating just until blended. Fill muffin cups $^2/_3$ full with batter.

3. Bake 15 to 18 minutes or until wooden pick inserted in center comes out clean. Remove from pan to wire rack. Cool completely. Prepare MOCHA GLAZE; drizzle over tops of brownie cups. Let stand until glaze is set. Store, covered, at room temperature.

Mocha Glaze

$^1/_4$ cup powdered sugar

$^3/_4$ teaspoon HERSHEY'S Cocoa

$^1/_4$ teaspoon powdered instant coffee

2 teaspoons hot water

$^1/_4$ teaspoon vanilla extract

Stir together powdered sugar and cocoa in small bowl. Dissolve instant coffee in water; gradually add to sugar mixture, stirring until well blended. Stir in vanilla.

Cinnamon Chips Gems

Makes 48 cookies

1 cup (2 sticks) butter or margarine, softened

2 packages (3 ounces each) cream cheese, softened

2 cups all-purpose flour

$1/2$ cup sugar

$1/3$ cup ground toasted almonds

2 eggs

1 can (14 ounces) sweetened condensed milk (not evaporated milk)

1 teaspoon vanilla extract

$1^1/_3$ cups HERSHEY'S Cinnamon Chips, divided

1. Beat butter and cream cheese in large bowl until well blended; stir in flour, sugar and almonds. Cover; refrigerate about 1 hour.

2. Divide dough into 4 equal parts. Shape each part into 12 smooth balls. Place each ball in small muffin cup ($1^3/_4$ inches in diameter); press evenly on bottom and up side of each cup.

3. Heat oven to 375°F. Beat eggs in small bowl. Add sweetened condensed milk and vanilla; mix well. Place 7 cinnamon chips in bottom of each cookie shell; fill a generous $3/_4$ full with sweetened condensed milk mixture.

4. Bake 18 to 20 minutes or until tops are puffed and just beginning to turn golden brown. Cool 3 minutes. Sprinkle about 15 chips on top of each cookie. Cool completely in pan on wire rack. Remove from pan using small metal spatula or sharp knife. Store tightly covered at room temperature.

Five Layer Bars

$^3/_4$ **cup (1$^1/_2$ sticks) butter or margarine**

1$^3/_4$ **cups graham cracker crumbs**

$^1/_4$ **cup HERSHEY'S Cocoa**

2 **tablespoons sugar**

1 **can (14 ounces) sweetened condensed milk (not evaporated milk)**

1 **cup HERSHEY'S SPECIAL DARK Chocolate Chips or HERSHEY'S Semi-Sweet Chocolate Chips**

1 **cup raisins, chopped dried apricots or miniature marshmallows**

1 **cup chopped nuts**

1. Heat oven to 350°F. Place butter in 13×9×2-inch baking pan. Heat in oven until melted; remove pan from oven.

2. Stir together crumbs, cocoa and sugar; sprinkle evenly over butter. Pour sweetened condensed milk evenly over crumb mixture. Sprinkle with chocolate chips and raisins. Sprinkle nuts on top; press down firmly.

3. Bake 25 to 30 minutes or until lightly browned. Cool completely in pan on wire rack. Cover with foil; let stand at room temperature 6 to 8 hours. Cut into bars.

Golden Bars: Substitute 1 cup REESE'S Peanut Butter Chips for chocolate chips. Sprinkle 1 cup golden raisins or chopped dried apricots over chips. Proceed as above.

Brownies, Bars & Cookies

Chunky Macadamia Bars

¾ **cup (1½ sticks) butter or margarine, softened**

1 **cup packed light brown sugar**

½ **cup granulated sugar**

1 **egg**

1 **teaspoon vanilla extract**

2¼ **cups all-purpose flour**

1 **teaspoon baking soda**

1¾ **cups (10-ounce package) HERSHEY'S MINI KISSES**BRAND **Milk Chocolates, divided**

¾ **cup MAUNA LOA Macadamia Baking Pieces**

VANILLA GLAZE (recipe follows)

1. Heat oven to 375°F.

2. Beat butter, brown sugar and granulated sugar in large bowl until fluffy. Add egg and vanilla; beat well. Add flour and baking soda; blend well. Stir in 1 cup chocolate pieces and nuts; press into ungreased 13×9×2-inch baking pan. Sprinkle with remaining ¾ cup chocolates.

3. Bake 22 to 25 minutes or until golden brown. Cool completely in pan on wire rack. Drizzle VANILLA GLAZE over top; allow to set. Cut into bars.

Vanilla Glaze: Combine 1 cup powdered sugar, 2 tablespoons milk and ½ teaspoon vanilla extract in small bowl; stir until smooth. Makes ⅓ cup glaze.

White Chip Lemon Streusel Bars

1 **can (14 ounces) sweetened condensed milk (not evaporated milk)**

$1/2$ **cup lemon juice**

1 **teaspoon freshly grated lemon peel**

2 **cups (12-ounce package) HERSHEY'S Premier White Chips, divided**

$2/3$ **cup butter or margarine, softened**

1 **cup packed light brown sugar**

$1^1/2$ **cups all-purpose flour**

$1^1/2$ **cups regular rolled or quick-cooking oats**

$3/4$ **cup toasted pecan pieces***

1 **teaspoon baking powder**

$1/2$ **teaspoon salt**

1 **egg**

$1/2$ **teaspoon shortening**

***To toast pecans:** Heat oven to 350°F. Spread pecans in thin layer in shallow baking pan. Bake, stirring occasionally, 7 to 8 minutes or until golden brown; cool.*

1. Heat oven to 350°F. Lightly grease 13×9×2-inch baking pan. Combine sweetened condensed milk, lemon juice and lemon peel in medium bowl; set aside. Measure out $1/4$ cup and $1/3$ cup white chips; set aside. Add remaining white chips to lemon mixture.

2. Beat butter and brown sugar with electric mixer on medium speed in large bowl until well blended. Stir together flour, oats, pecans, baking powder and salt; add to butter mixture, blending well. Set aside $1^2/3$ cups oats mixture. Add egg to remaining oats mixture, blending until crumbly; press onto bottom of prepared pan. Gently spoon lemon mixture on top, spreading evenly. Add reserved $1/3$ cup white chips to reserved oats mixture. Sprinkle over lemon layer, pressing down lightly.

3. Bake 20 to 25 minutes or until lightly browned. Cool in pan on wire rack. Place remaining $1/4$ cup white chips and shortening in small microwave-safe bowl. Microwave at MEDIUM (50%) 30 seconds or until chips are melted and mixture is smooth when stirred. Drizzle over baked bars. Allow drizzle to set; cut into bars.

Double-Drizzled Chocolate Shortbread Cookies

Makes about 72 cookies

2 cups (4 sticks) butter or margarine, softened

1¹/₃ cups sugar

1 teaspoon vanilla extract

4 egg yolks

4 cups all-purpose flour

¹/₂ cup HERSHEY'S SPECIAL DARK Cocoa

1 teaspoon salt

1 cup chopped pecans

1 cup HERSHEY'S SPECIAL DARK Chocolate Chips or HERSHEY'S Semi-Sweet Chocolate Chips

2 tablespoons shortening (do not use butter, margarine, spread or oil), divided

1 cup REESE'S Peanut Butter Chips or HERSHEY'S Premier White Chips

1. Beat butter, sugar and vanilla until well blended. Add egg yolks, one at a time, beating well after each addition. Gradually add flour, cocoa and salt, beating until blended. (Batter is very stiff.)

2. Divide dough in half. Shape each part into 12-inch-long log. Roll each in pecans, pressing firmly to have pecans adhere. Wrap each roll separately in plastic wrap. Refrigerate 6 to 8 hours.

3. Heat oven to 350°F. Using a sharp knife, cut rolls into ³/₈-inch slices. Place on ungreased cookie sheet. Bake 10 to 12 minutes or until set. Cool slightly. Remove from cookie sheet to wire rack. Cool completely.

4. Place chocolate chips and 1 tablespoon shortening in small microwave-safe bowl. Microwave at MEDIUM (50%) 1 minute; stir. If necessary, microwave at MEDIUM an additional 15 seconds at a time, stirring after each heating, until chips are melted and smooth when stirred. Drizzle over tops of cookies. Melt peanut butter chips or white chips with remaining 1 tablespoon shortening; drizzle over chocolate. Let stand until drizzles are set.

Secret KISSES® Cookies

1 cup (2 sticks) butter or margarine, softened

$1/2$ cup granulated sugar

1 teaspoon vanilla extract

$1^3/_4$ cups all-purpose flour

1 cup finely chopped walnuts or almonds

36 HERSHEY'S KISSES BRAND Milk Chocolates or HERSHEY'S KISSES BRAND Milk Chocolates with Almonds

Powdered sugar

1. Beat butter, granulated sugar and vanilla with electric mixer on medium speed in large bowl until fluffy. Add flour and walnuts; beat on low speed of mixer until well blended. Cover; refrigerate 1 to 2 hours or until dough is firm enough to handle.

2. Remove wrappers from chocolates. Heat oven to 375°F. Using about 1 tablespoon dough for each cookie, shape dough around each chocolate; roll in hand to make ball. (Be sure to cover each chocolate piece completely.) Place on ungreased cookie sheet.

3. Bake 10 to 12 minutes or until cookies are set but not browned. Cool slightly; remove to wire rack. While still slightly warm, roll in powdered sugar. Cool completely. Store in tightly covered container. Roll again in powdered sugar just before serving.

Variation: Sift together 1 tablespoon HERSHEY'S Cocoa with $1/3$ cup powdered sugar. Roll warm cookies in cocoa mixture.

MINI KISSES® Fruit Bars

$1^1/_2$ **cups all-purpose flour**

$1^1/_2$ **cups quick-cooking rolled oats**

1 **cup packed light brown sugar**

1 **teaspoon baking powder**

$^3/_4$ **cup ($1^1/_2$ sticks) butter or margarine, softened**

1 **jar (10 to 12 ounces) raspberry jam**

$1^3/_4$ **cups (10-ounce package) HERSHEY'S MINI KISSES**BRAND **Milk Chocolates**

$^1/_2$ **cup chopped nuts (optional)**

1. Heat oven to 350°F. Lightly grease 13×9×2-inch baking pan.

2. Combine flour, oats, brown sugar and baking powder in large bowl. Cut butter into flour mixture with pastry blender or two knives until crumbly. Remove 2 cups crumb mixture; set aside.

3. Press remaining crumb mixture onto bottom of prepared pan. Stir jam to soften; carefully spread over crumb mixture. Sprinkle chocolates evenly over jam. Cover with reserved crumbs. Sprinkle nuts over top, if desired; press firmly.

4. Bake 40 to 45 minutes or until lightly browned. Cool completely in pan on wire rack. Cut into bars.

Almond Shortbread Cookies with Chocolate Filling

Makes about 44 sandwich cookies

$^3/_4$ **cup sliced almonds, toasted***

1 **cup (2 sticks) butter or margarine, softened**

$^3/_4$ **cup granulated sugar**

3 **egg yolks**

$^3/_4$ **teaspoon almond extract**

2 **cups all-purpose flour**

CHOCOLATE FILLING (recipe follows)

Powdered sugar (optional)

***To toast almonds:** Heat oven to 350°F. Spread almonds in thin layer in shallow baking pan. Bake 8 to 10 minutes, stirring occasionally, until light golden brown; cool.*

1. Finely chop almonds; set aside.

2. Beat butter and granulated sugar in large bowl until creamy. Add egg yolks and almond extract; beat well. Gradually add flour, beating until well blended. Stir in almonds. Refrigerate dough 1 to 2 hours or until firm enough to handle.

3. Heat oven to 350°F. On well-floured surface, roll about $^1/_4$ of dough to about $^1/_8$-inch thickness (keep remaining dough in refrigerator). Using 2-inch round cookie cutter, cut into equal number of rounds. Place on ungreased cookie sheet. Repeat with remaining dough.

4. Bake 8 to 10 minutes or until almost set. Cool slightly; remove from cookie sheet to wire rack. Cool completely. Spread about 1 measuring teaspoonful CHOCOLATE FILLING onto bottom of one cookie. Top with second cookie; gently press together. Repeat with remaining cookies. Allow to set, about 1 hour. Lightly sift powdered sugar over top of cookies, if desired. Cover; store at room temperature.

Chocolate Filling: Combine 1 cup HERSHEY'S Milk Chocolate Chips** and $^1/_3$ cup whipping cream in small saucepan. Stir constantly over low heat until mixture is smooth. Remove from heat. Cool about 20 minutes or until slightly thickened and spreadable. Makes about 1 cup filling.

***HERSHEY'S SPECIAL DARK Chocolate Chips or HERSHEY'S Semi-Sweet Chocolate Chips may also be used.*

Brownies, Bars & Cookies

Best Fudgey Pecan Brownies

$1/2$ **cup (1 stick) butter or margarine, melted**

1 **cup sugar**

1 **teaspoon vanilla extract**

2 **eggs**

$1/2$ **cup all-purpose flour**

$1/3$ **cup HERSHEY'S Cocoa**

$1/4$ **teaspoon baking powder**

$1/4$ **teaspoon salt**

$1/2$ **cup coarsely chopped pecans**

CHOCOLATE PECAN FROSTING (recipe follows)

Pecan halves

1. Heat oven to 350°F. Lightly grease 8- or 9-inch baking pan.

2. Beat butter, sugar and vanilla with spoon in large bowl. Add eggs; beat well. Stir together flour, cocoa, baking powder and salt; gradually add to egg mixture, beating until well blended. Stir in chopped pecans. Spread in prepared pan.

3. Bake 20 to 25 minutes or until brownies begin to pull away from sides of pan. Meanwhile, prepare CHOCOLATE PECAN FROSTING. Spread warm frosting over warm brownies. Garnish with pecan halves. Cool completely; cut into squares.

Chocolate Pecan Frosting

$1^{1}/3$ **cups powdered sugar**

2 **tablespoons HERSHEY'S Cocoa**

3 **tablespoons butter or margarine**

2 **tablespoons milk**

$1/4$ **teaspoon vanilla extract**

$1/4$ **cup chopped pecans**

1. Stir together powdered sugar and cocoa in medium bowl.

2. Heat butter and milk in small saucepan over low heat until butter is melted. Gradually beat into cocoa mixture, beating until smooth. Stir in vanilla and pecans.

Makes about 1 cup frosting

Chocolate Macaroon Bars

Makes 24 to 36 bars

1¼ **cups graham cracker crumbs**

⅓ **cup sugar**

¼ **cup HERSHEY'S Cocoa**

⅓ **cup butter or margarine, melted**

1 **can (14 ounces) sweetened condensed milk (not evaporated milk)**

2⅔ **cups MOUNDS Sweetened Coconut Flakes**

2 **cups fresh white bread crumbs (about 5 slices)**

2 **eggs**

2 **teaspoons vanilla extract**

1 **cup HERSHEY'S Mini Chips Semi-Sweet Chocolate**

1. Heat oven to 350°F.

2. Stir together graham cracker crumbs, sugar, cocoa and butter in large bowl; press firmly onto bottom of ungreased 13×9×2-inch baking pan.

3. Bake 10 minutes. Meanwhile, combine sweetened condensed milk, coconut, bread crumbs, eggs, vanilla and small chocolate chips in large bowl; stir until blended. Spoon over prepared crust, spreading evenly.

4. Bake 30 minutes or until lightly browned. Cool completely in pan on wire rack. Cut into bars. Store covered in refrigerator.

Toffee Studded Snickerdoodles

Makes about 60 cookies

¹/₂ **cup (1 stick) butter or margarine, softened**

¹/₂ **cup shortening**

1¹/₃ **cups sugar, divided**

2 **eggs**

2³/₄ **cups all-purpose flour**

2 **teaspoons cream of tartar**

1 **teaspoon baking soda**

¹/₄ **teaspoon salt**

1¹/₃ **cups (8-ounce package) HEATH BITS 'O BRICKLE Toffee Bits**

2 **teaspoons ground cinnamon**

1. Heat oven to 400°F.

2. Beat butter, shortening and 1 cup sugar in large bowl until fluffy. Add eggs; beat thoroughly. Stir together flour, cream of tartar, baking soda and salt; gradually add to butter mixture, beating until well blended. Stir in toffee bits.

3. Stir together remaining ¹/₃ cup sugar and cinnamon. Shape dough into 1¹/₄-inch balls; roll in sugar-cinnamon mixture. Place on ungreased cookie sheets.

4. Bake 9 to 11 minutes or until lightly browned around edges. Cool 1 minute; remove from cookie sheets to wire racks. Cool completely.

KISSES® Macaroon Cookies

1/3 cup butter or margarine, softened

1 package (3 ounces) cream cheese, softened

3/4 cup sugar

1 egg yolk

2 teaspoons almond extract

2 teaspoons orange juice

1 1/4 cups all-purpose flour

2 teaspoons baking powder

1/4 teaspoon salt

5 cups MOUNDS Sweetened Coconut Flakes, divided

48 HERSHEY'S KISSES BRAND Milk Chocolates

1. Beat butter, cream cheese and sugar with electric mixer on medium speed in large bowl until well blended. Add egg yolk, almond extract and orange juice; beat well. Stir together flour, baking powder and salt; gradually add to butter mixture. Stir in 3 cups coconut. Cover; refrigerate 1 hour or until firm enough to handle. Meanwhile, remove wrappers from chocolates.

2. Heat oven to 350°F.

3. Shape dough into 1-inch balls; roll in remaining 2 cups coconut. Place on ungreased cookie sheet.

4. Bake 10 to 12 minutes or until lightly browned. Immediately press chocolate piece into center of each cookie. Cool 1 minute. Carefully remove to wire rack and cool completely.

Grandma's Favorite Sugarcakes

²/₃ **cup butter or margarine, softened**

1¹/₂ **cups packed light brown sugar**

1 **cup granulated sugar**

2 **eggs**

2 **teaspoons vanilla extract**

4¹/₂ **cups all-purpose flour**

2 **teaspoons baking soda**

1 **teaspoon baking powder**

1 **teaspoon salt**

1 **cup buttermilk or sour milk***

2 **cups (12-ounce package) HERSHEY'S Mini Chips Semi-Sweet Chocolate**

2 **cups chopped walnuts or pecans**

Vanilla frosting (optional)

Colored sugar or sprinkles (optional)

***To sour milk:** Use 1 tablespoon white vinegar plus milk to equal 1 cup.*

1. Heat oven to 350°F. Grease cookie sheet or line with parchment paper.

2. Beat butter, brown sugar and granulated sugar until well blended in large mixing bowl. Add eggs and vanilla; beat until creamy. Stir together flour, baking soda, baking powder and salt; add alternately with buttermilk to butter mixture, beating well after each addition. Stir in chocolate chips and nuts. Drop by level ¹/₄ cups or heaping tablespoons 2 inches apart onto prepared cookie sheet.

3. Bake 12 to 14 minutes or until golden brown. Cool slightly; remove to wire rack. Cool completely. Frost with favorite vanilla frosting; garnish with colored sugar, if desired.

Brownies, Bars & Cookies

Oatmeal Toffee Cookies

1 cup (2 sticks) butter or margarine, softened

2 cups packed light brown sugar

2 eggs

2 teaspoons vanilla extract

1$^3/_4$ cups all-purpose flour

1 teaspoon baking soda

1 teaspoon ground cinnamon

$^1/_2$ teaspoon salt

3 cups quick-cooking oats

1$^1/_3$ cups (8-ounce package) **HEATH BITS 'O BRICKLE Toffee Bits**

1 cup **MOUNDS** Sweetened Coconut Flakes (optional)

1. Heat oven to 375°F. Lightly grease cookie sheet or line with parchment paper.

2. Beat butter, brown sugar, eggs and vanilla with electric mixer on medium speed in large bowl until well blended. Add flour, baking soda, cinnamon and salt; beat until blended. Stir in oats, toffee bits and coconut, if desired, with spoon. Drop dough by rounded teaspoons about 2 inches apart onto prepared cookie sheet.

3. Bake 8 to 10 minutes or until edges are lightly browned. Cool 1 minute. Remove to wire rack and cool completely.

Chewy Drizzled Cinnamon Chip Cookies

Makes about 60 cookies

3/4 cup (1 1/2 sticks) butter or margarine, softened

1 cup packed light brown sugar

1/4 cup light corn syrup

1 egg

1 2/3 cups (10-ounce package) HERSHEY'S Cinnamon Chips, divided

2 1/2 cups all-purpose flour

2 teaspoons baking soda

1/4 teaspoon salt

1 cup finely ground pecans or walnuts

CINNAMON CHIPS DRIZZLE (recipe follows)

1. Beat butter and brown sugar in large bowl until fluffy. Add corn syrup and egg; mix well.

2. Place 1 cup cinnamon chips in microwave-safe bowl. Microwave at MEDIUM (50%) 1 minute; stir. If necessary, microwave at MEDIUM an additional 15 seconds at a time, stirring after each heating, just until chips are melted when stirred. Stir melted chips into butter mixture.

3. Stir together flour, baking soda and salt; add to cinnamon chips mixture, beating just until blended. Cover; refrigerate dough about 1 hour or until firm enough to handle.

4. Heat oven to 350°F. Shape dough into 1-inch balls; roll in nuts, lightly pressing nuts into dough. Place on ungreased cookie sheet.

5. Bake 8 to 10 minutes or until golden around edges. Cool slightly; remove from cookie sheet to wire rack. Cool completely. Drizzle with CINNAMON CHIPS DRIZZLE.

Cinnamon Chips Drizzle: Place remaining 2/3 cup cinnamon chips and 1 1/2 teaspoons shortening (do not use butter, margarine, spread or oil) in small microwave-safe bowl. Microwave at MEDIUM (50%) 1 minute; stir until chips are melted and mixture is smooth.

Toffee & Coconut Peanut Butter Crisscrosses

Makes about 78 cookies

3/4 **cup REESE'S Creamy Peanut Butter**

1/2 **cup shortening**

1/3 **cup granulated sugar**

1/3 **cup packed light brown sugar**

1 **egg**

2 **tablespoons milk**

1 **teaspoon vanilla extract**

1 1/2 **cups all-purpose flour**

1 **teaspoon baking soda**

1/2 **teaspoon salt**

1 1/3 **cups (8-ounce package) HEATH BITS 'O BRICKLE Toffee Bits**

1 **cup MOUNDS Sweetened Coconut Flakes**

1. Heat oven to 375°F.

2. Beat peanut butter and shortening in large bowl until well blended. Add granulated sugar and brown sugar; beat until fluffy. Add egg, milk and vanilla; beat well. Stir together flour, baking soda and salt; gradually beat into peanut butter mixture. Stir in toffee bits and coconut.

3. Shape dough into 1-inch balls. Place on ungreased cookie sheet. With tines of fork, flatten ball. Flatten again in opposite direction, forming crisscross marks.

4. Bake 8 to 10 minutes or until edges of cookies are golden brown. Cool slightly; remove from cookie sheet to wire rack. Cool completely.

Butterscotch Blondies

$^3/_4$ **cup ($1^1/_2$ sticks) butter or margarine, softened**

$^3/_4$ **cup packed light brown sugar**

$^1/_2$ **cup granulated sugar**

2 **eggs**

2 **cups all-purpose flour**

1 **teaspoon baking soda**

$^1/_2$ **teaspoon salt**

$1^3/_4$ **cups (11-ounce package) HERSHEY'S Butterscotch Chips**

1 **cup chopped nuts (optional)**

1. Heat oven to 350°F. Grease 13×9×2-inch baking pan.

2. Beat butter, brown sugar and granulated sugar in large bowl until creamy. Add eggs; beat well. Stir together flour, baking soda and salt; gradually add to butter mixture, blending well. Stir in butterscotch chips and nuts, if desired. Spread in prepared pan.

3. Bake 30 to 35 minutes or until top is golden brown and center is set. Cool completely in pan on wire rack. Cut into bars.

HERSHEY'S® Mint Chocolate Chip Cookies

³/₄ cup (1¹/₂ sticks) butter or margarine, softened

1 cup sugar

1 egg

1 teaspoon vanilla extract

1¹/₂ cups all-purpose flour

¹/₂ teaspoon baking soda

¹/₄ teaspoon salt

1²/₃ cups (10-ounce package) HERSHEY'S Mint Chocolate Chips

1. Heat oven to 350°F.

2. Beat butter and sugar in large bowl until fluffy. Add egg and vanilla; beat well. Stir together flour, baking soda and salt; gradually blend into butter mixture. Stir in mint chocolate chips. Drop by rounded teaspoons onto ungreased cookie sheet.

3. Bake 10 to 12 minutes or just until lightly browned. Cool slightly; remove from cookie sheet to wire rack. Cool completely.

Cakes
&
Cheesecakes

Chocolate Cappuccino Cream Cake

Makes 12 to 16 servings

27 ladyfingers, split

3 packages (3 ounces each) cream cheese, softened and divided

²/₃ cup plus 2 tablespoons HERSHEY'S Syrup or HERSHEY'S SPECIAL DARK Syrup, divided

¹/₃ cup water

5¹/₄ cups frozen whipped topping, thawed and divided

¹/₂ cup cold brewed coffee

1. Line 9-inch springform pan with foil; place ladyfingers, cut side in, to fit on bottom and around sides of prepared pan.

2. Beat half of cream cheese until fluffy in medium bowl; gradually blend in ²/₃ cup chocolate syrup and ¹/₃ cup water until smooth. Fold in 2¹/₂ cups topping until blended; spread evenly over ladyfingers. Cut rounded ends off remaining ladyfingers; place to fit over top of chocolate layer.

3. Beat remaining half of cream cheese until fluffy in medium bowl; gradually blend in cold coffee and remaining 2 tablespoons chocolate syrup. Fold in remaining 2³/₄ cups topping until blended; spread evenly over ladyfingers. Cover; freeze 6 hours or until firm.

4. Remove foil; garnish, if desired. Serve frozen, cut into slices.

Cinnamon Chip Applesauce Coffee Cake

1 cup (2 sticks) butter or margarine, softened

1 cup granulated sugar

2 eggs

$1/2$ teaspoon vanilla extract

$3/4$ cup applesauce

$2^1/2$ cups all-purpose flour

1 teaspoon baking soda

$1/2$ teaspoon salt

$1^2/3$ cups (10-ounce package) HERSHEY'S Cinnamon Chips

1 cup chopped pecans (optional)

$3/4$ cup powdered sugar

1 to 2 tablespoons warm water

1. Heat oven to 350°F. Lightly grease 13×9×2-inch baking pan.

2. Beat butter and granulated sugar with electric mixer on medium speed in large bowl until well blended. Beat in eggs and vanilla. Mix in applesauce. Stir together flour, baking soda and salt; gradually add to butter mixture, beating until well blended. Stir in cinnamon chips and pecans, if desired. Spread in prepared pan.

3. Bake 30 to 35 minutes or until wooden pick inserted in center comes out clean. Cool in pan on wire rack. Sprinkle cake with powdered sugar or stir together $3/4$ cup powdered sugar and warm water to make smooth glaze; drizzle over cake. Serve at room temperature or while still slightly warm.

Fluted Cake: Grease and flour 12-cup fluted tube pan. Prepare batter as directed; pour into prepared pan. Bake 45 to 50 minutes or until wooden pick inserted in thickest part comes out clean. Cool 15 minutes; invert onto wire rack. Cool completely.

Cupcakes: Line 24 baking cups ($2^1/2$ inches in diameter) with paper bake cups. Prepare batter as directed; divide evenly into prepared cups. Bake 15 to 18 minutes or until wooden pick inserted in center comes out clean. Cool completely.

Cakes & Cheesecakes

56

HERSHEY'S® "Perfectly Chocolate" Chocolate Cake

2 cups sugar

1³/₄ cups all-purpose flour

³/₄ cup HERSHEY'S Cocoa

1¹/₂ teaspoons baking powder

1¹/₂ teaspoons baking soda

1 teaspoon salt

2 eggs

1 cup milk

¹/₂ cup vegetable oil

2 teaspoons vanilla extract

1 cup boiling water

"PERFECTLY CHOCOLATE"
CHOCOLATE FROSTING
(recipe follows)

1. Heat oven to 350°F. Grease and flour two 9-inch round baking pans.

2. Stir together sugar, flour, cocoa, baking powder, baking soda and salt in large bowl. Add eggs, milk, oil and vanilla; beat on medium speed of mixer 2 minutes. Stir in boiling water (batter will be thin). Pour batter evenly into prepared pans.

3. Bake 30 to 35 minutes or until wooden pick inserted into center comes out clean. Cool 10 minutes; remove from pans to wire racks. Cool completely. Frost with "PERFECTLY CHOCOLATE" CHOCOLATE FROSTING.

One-Pan Cake: Grease and flour 13×9×2-inch baking pan. Heat oven to 350°F. Pour batter into prepared pan. Bake 35 to 40 minutes. Cool completely. Frost.

Three Layer Cake: Grease and flour three 8-inch round baking pans. Heat oven to 350°F. Pour batter into prepared pans. Bake 30 to 35 minutes. Cool 10 minutes; remove from pans to wire racks. Cool completely. Frost.

Bundt Cake: Grease and flour 12-cup fluted tube pan. Heat oven to 350°F. Pour batter into prepared pan. Bake 50 to 55 minutes. Cool 15 minutes; remove from pan to wire rack. Cool completely. Frost.

Cupcakes: Line muffin cups (2¹/₂ inches in diameter) with paper bake cups. Heat oven to 350°F. Fill cups ²/₃ full with batter. Bake 22 to 25 minutes. Cool completely. Frost. Makes about 30 cupcakes.

Cakes & Cheesecakes

"Perfectly Chocolate" Chocolate Frosting

- ¹/₂ **cup (1 stick) butter or margarine**
- ²/₃ **cup HERSHEY'S Cocoa**
- 3 **cups powdered sugar**
- ¹/₃ **cup milk**
- 1 **teaspoon vanilla extract**

Melt butter. Stir in cocoa. Alternately add powdered sugar and milk, beating to spreading consistency. Add small amount additional milk, if needed. Stir in vanilla.

Makes about 2 cups frosting

White Chip and Macadamia Nut Coffee Cake

CRUMB TOPPING (recipe follows)

6 **tablespoons butter or margarine, softened**

$^3/_4$ **cup granulated sugar**

$^3/_4$ **cup packed light brown sugar**

2 **cups all-purpose flour**

2 **teaspoons baking powder**

$^1/_2$ **teaspoon ground cinnamon**

$1^1/_4$ **cups milk**

1 **egg**

1 **teaspoon vanilla extract**

WHITE DRIZZLE (recipe follows)

1. Heat oven to 350°F. Grease and flour 13×9×2-inch baking pan. Prepare CRUMB TOPPING; set aside.

2. Beat butter, granulated sugar and brown sugar until well blended. Stir together flour, baking powder and cinnamon; beat into butter mixture. Gradually add milk, egg and vanilla, beating until thoroughly blended. Pour $^1/_2$ batter into prepared pan; top with $^1/_2$ CRUMB TOPPING. Gently spread remaining batter over topping. Sprinkle remaining topping over batter.

3. Bake 30 to 35 minutes or until wooden pick inserted in center comes out clean. Cool completely.

4. Prepare WHITE DRIZZLE; drizzle over cake.

Crumb Topping: Combine $^2/_3$ cup packed light brown sugar, $^1/_2$ cup all-purpose flour, 6 tablespoons firm butter or margarine, 1 cup HERSHEY'S Premier White Chips and $^1/_2$ cup MAUNA LOA Macadamia Nut Baking Pieces in medium bowl. Mix until crumbly.

White Drizzle: Beat together $^3/_4$ cup powdered sugar, 2 to 3 teaspoons milk, 1 teaspoon softened butter and $^1/_4$ teaspoon vanilla extract. If necessary, stir in additional milk, $^1/_2$ teaspoon at a time, until desired consistency.

Cakes & Cheesecakes

Cheesecake 5 Ways

CRUMB CRUST (recipe follows)

3 packages (8 ounces each) cream cheese, softened

³/₄ cup sugar

3 eggs

1 teaspoon vanilla extract

1. Prepare CRUMB CRUST. Heat oven to 350°F.

2. Beat cream cheese and sugar in large bowl until smooth. Add eggs, one at a time, beating well after each addition. Stir in vanilla. Pour into prepared crust.

3. Bake 45 to 50 minutes or until almost set.* Remove from oven to wire rack. With knife, loosen cake from side of pan. Cool completely; remove side of pan.

4. Cover; refrigerate several hours or until chilled. Just before serving, garnish as desired. Cover and refrigerate leftover cheesecake.

Cheesecakes are less likely to crack if baked in a water bath.

Crumb Crust: Heat oven to 350°F. Stir together 1 cup graham cracker crumbs and 2 tablespoons sugar in small bowl; blend in ¹/₄ cup (¹/₂ stick) melted butter or margarine, mixing well. Press mixture onto bottom and ¹/₂ inch up side of 9-inch springform pan. Bake 8 to 10 minutes. Cool.

Chocolate Cheesecake: Increase sugar to 1¹/₄ cups and add ¹/₃ cup HERSHEY'S Cocoa. Increase vanilla extract to 1¹/₂ teaspoons.

Toffee Bits Cheesecake: Prepare cheesecake as directed. Stir 1¹/₃ cups (8-ounce package) HEATH BITS 'O BRICKLE Toffee Bits into batter.

Chocolate Chip Cheesecake: Prepare cheesecake as directed. Stir 1 to 1¹/₂ cups HERSHEY'S Mini Chips Semi-Sweet Chocolate into batter.

Mocha Cheesecake: Prepare Chocolate Cheesecake, using HERSHEY'S SPECIAL DARK Cocoa. Add 1¹/₂ teaspoons powdered instant coffee to batter.

Mocha Toffee with Chocolate Chips Cheesecake: Prepare Mocha Cheesecake as directed. Stir ³/₄ cup HEATH BITS 'O BRICKLE Toffee Bits and ³/₄ cup HERSHEY'S Mini Chips Semi-Sweet Chocolate into batter.

Mocha Cheesecake

Creamy Cinnamon Chips Cheesecake

Makes 12 to 14 servings

1½ **cups graham cracker crumbs**

1 **cup plus 2 tablespoons sugar, divided**

5 **tablespoons butter, melted**

2 **packages (8 ounces each) cream cheese, softened**

1 **teaspoon vanilla extract**

3 **cartons (8 ounces each) dairy sour cream**

3 **eggs, slightly beaten**

1⅔ **cups (10-ounce package) HERSHEY'S Cinnamon Chips, divided**

1 **teaspoon shortening (do not use butter, margarine, spread or oil)**

1. Heat oven to 325°F. Combine graham cracker crumbs, 2 tablespoons sugar and melted butter in medium bowl. Press crumb mixture evenly onto bottom and about 1½ inches up side of 9-inch springform pan. Bake 8 minutes. Remove from oven.

2. Increase oven temperature to 350°F. Beat cream cheese, remaining 1 cup sugar and vanilla on medium speed of mixer until well blended. Add sour cream; beat on low speed until blended. Add eggs; beat on low speed just until blended. Do not overbeat.

3. Pour half of filling into prepared crust. Sprinkle 1⅓ cups chips evenly over filling in pan. Carefully spoon remaining filling over chips. Place on shallow baking pan.

4. Bake about 1 hour or until center is almost set. Remove from oven; cool 10 minutes on wire rack. Using knife or narrow metal spatula, loosen cheesecake from side of pan. Cool on wire rack 30 minutes more. Remove side of pan; cool 1 hour.

5. Combine shortening and remaining ⅓ cup chips in small microwave-safe bowl. Microwave at MEDIUM (50%) 30 seconds; stir until chips are melted. Drizzle over cheesecake; cover and refrigerate at least 4 hours. Cover and refrigerate leftover cheesecake.

Dandy Cake

1 cup water

1 cup (2 sticks) butter or
   margarine

$^1/_3$ cup HERSHEY'S Cocoa

2 cups all-purpose flour

2 cups sugar

1 teaspoon baking soda

$^1/_2$ teaspoon salt

3 eggs

$^3/_4$ cup dairy sour cream

$^3/_4$ cup REESE'S Creamy Peanut
   Butter

   CHOCOLATE TOPPING
   (recipe follows)

1. Heat oven to 350°F. Grease and flour 15$^1/_2$×10$^1/_2$×1-inch jelly-roll pan.

2. Combine water, butter and cocoa in small saucepan. Cook over medium heat, stirring occasionally, until mixture boils; boil and stir 1 minute. Remove from heat; set aside.

3. Stir together flour, sugar, baking soda and salt in large bowl. Add eggs and sour cream; beat until well blended. Add cocoa mixture; beat just until blended (batter will be thin). Pour into prepared pan.

4. Bake 25 to 30 minutes or until wooden pick inserted in center comes out clean. Do not remove cake from pan. Spread peanut butter over warm cake. Cool completely in pan on wire rack. Prepare CHOCOLATE TOPPING; carefully spread over top, covering peanut butter. Allow topping to set; cut into squares.

Chocolate Topping: Place 2 cups (12-ounce package) HERSHEY'S SPECIAL DARK Chocolate Chips or HERSHEY'S Semi-Sweet Chocolate Chips and 2 tablespoons shortening (do not use butter, margarine, spread or oil) in small microwave-safe bowl. Microwave at MEDIUM (50%) 1$^1/_2$ minutes; stir. If necessary, microwave at MEDIUM an additional 15 seconds at a time, stirring after each heating, just until chips are melted when stirred.

Chilled Raspberry Cheesecake

1½ **cups vanilla wafer crumbs (about 45 wafers, crushed)**

⅓ **cup HERSHEY'S Cocoa**

⅓ **cup powdered sugar**

⅓ **cup butter or margarine, melted**

1 **package (10 ounces) frozen raspberries (about 2½ cups), thawed**

1 **envelope unflavored gelatin**

½ **cup cold water**

½ **cup boiling water**

2 **packages (8 ounces each) cream cheese, softened**

½ **cup granulated sugar**

1 **teaspoon vanilla extract**

3 **tablespoons seedless red raspberry preserves**

CHOCOLATE WHIPPED CREAM (recipe follows)

Fresh raspberries (optional)

Mint leaves (optional)

1. Heat oven to 350°F.

2. Stir together vanilla wafer crumbs, ⅓ cup cocoa and ⅓ cup powdered sugar in medium bowl; stir in melted butter. Press mixture onto bottom and 1½ inches up side of 9-inch springform pan. Bake 10 minutes; cool completely.

3. Purée and strain raspberries; set aside. Sprinkle gelatin over cold water in small bowl; let stand several minutes to soften. Add boiling water; stir until gelatin dissolves completely and mixture is clear. Beat cream cheese, granulated sugar and 1 teaspoon vanilla in large bowl until smooth. Gradually add raspberry purée and gelatin, mixing thoroughly; pour into prepared crust.

4. Refrigerate several hours or overnight. Loosen cake from side of pan with knife; remove side of pan. Stir raspberry preserves to soften; spread over cheesecake top. Garnish with CHOCOLATE WHIPPED CREAM, raspberries and mint, if desired. Cover; refrigerate leftovers.

Chocolate Whipped Cream: Stir together ½ cup powdered sugar and ¼ cup HERSHEY'S Cocoa in medium bowl. Add 1 cup (½ pint) cold whipping cream and 1 teaspoon vanilla extract; beat until stiff.

Chocolate Glazed Citrus Poppy Seed Cake

1 package (about 18 ounces)
   lemon cake mix

$^1/_3$ cup poppy seed

$^1/_3$ cup milk

3 eggs

1 cup plain lowfat yogurt

1 teaspoon freshly grated
   lemon peel

   CHOCOLATE CITRUS GLAZE
   (recipe follows)

1. Heat oven to 350°F. Grease and flour 12-cup fluted tube pan or 10-inch tube pan.

2. Combine cake mix, poppy seed, milk, eggs, yogurt and lemon peel in large bowl; beat until well blended. Pour batter into prepared pan.

3. Bake 40 to 45 minutes or until wooden pick inserted in center comes out clean. Cool 20 minutes; remove from pan to wire rack. Cool completely.

4. Prepare CHOCOLATE CITRUS GLAZE; spoon over cake, allowing glaze to run down sides.

Chocolate Citrus Glaze

2 tablespoons butter or
   margarine

2 tablespoons HERSHEY'S
   Cocoa or HERSHEY'S
   SPECIAL DARK Cocoa

2 tablespoons water

1 tablespoon orange-flavored
   liqueur (optional)

$^1/_2$ teaspoon orange extract

$1^1/_4$ to $1^1/_2$ cups powdered sugar

Melt butter in small saucepan over medium heat; remove from heat. Stir in cocoa, water, liqueur, if desired, and orange extract. Whisk in $1^1/_4$ cups powdered sugar until smooth. If glaze is too thin, whisk in remaining $^1/_4$ cup powdered sugar. Use immediately.

HERSHEY'S® KISSES® Birthday Cake

2 cups sugar

1³/₄ cups all-purpose flour

³/₄ cup HERSHEY'S Cocoa or HERSHEY'S SPECIAL DARK Cocoa

1¹/₂ teaspoons baking powder

1¹/₂ teaspoons baking soda

1 teaspoon salt

2 eggs

1 cup milk

¹/₂ cup vegetable oil

2 teaspoons vanilla extract

1 cup boiling water

VANILLA BUTTERCREAM FROSTING (recipe follows)

HERSHEY'S KISSESBRAND Milk Chocolates

1. Heat oven to 350°F. Grease and flour two (9-inch) round baking pans or one (13×9×2-inch) baking pan.

2. Stir together sugar, flour, cocoa, baking powder, baking soda and salt in large bowl. Add eggs, milk, oil and vanilla; beat with electric mixer on medium speed for 2 minutes. Stir in boiling water (batter will be thin). Pour batter into prepared pans.

3. Bake 30 to 35 minutes for round pans, 35 to 40 minutes for rectangular pan or until wooden pick inserted in center comes out clean. Cool 10 minutes; turn out onto wire racks. Cool completely.

4. Frost with VANILLA BUTTERCREAM FROSTING. Remove wrappers from chocolates. Garnish top and sides of cake with chocolates.

Vanilla Buttercream Frosting

¹/₃ cup butter or margarine, softened

4 cups powdered sugar, divided

3 to 4 tablespoons milk

1¹/₂ teaspoons vanilla extract

Beat butter with electric mixer on medium speed in large bowl until creamy. With mixer running, gradually add about 2 cups powdered sugar, beating until well blended. Slowly beat in milk and vanilla. Gradually add remaining powdered sugar, beating until smooth. Add additional milk, if necessary, until frosting is desired consistency.

Makes about 2¹/₃ cups frosting

Creamy Ambrosia Cheesecake

1$^1/_3$ cups graham cracker crumbs

$^1/_2$ cup MOUNDS Sweetened Coconut Flakes

$^1/_4$ cup ($^1/_2$ stick) melted butter or margarine

1$^1/_4$ cups plus 2 tablespoons sugar, divided

1 can (11 ounces) mandarin orange segments

1 can (8 ounces) crushed pineapple in juice

3 packages (8 ounces each) cream cheese, softened

3 eggs

2 cups (12-ounce package) HERSHEY'S Premier White Chips

TROPICAL FRUIT SAUCE (recipe follows)

Additional MOUNDS Sweetened Coconut Flakes

1. Heat oven to 350°F. Stir graham cracker crumbs, coconut, melted butter and 2 tablespoons sugar in medium bowl. Press mixture firmly onto bottom of 9-inch springform pan. Bake 8 minutes; cool slightly. Drain oranges and pineapple, reserving juices. Chop oranges into small pieces.

2. Beat cream cheese in large bowl until fluffy. Add remaining 1$^1/_4$ cups sugar; beat well. Add eggs; beat well. Stir in white chips, oranges and pineapple. Pour mixture over crust.

3. Bake 60 to 65 minutes or until center is almost set. Remove from oven to wire rack. With knife, loosen cake from side of pan. Cool completely; remove side of pan. Cover; refrigerate until cold. Garnish with additional coconut, if desired, and serve with TROPICAL FRUIT SAUCE. Cover and refrigerate leftovers.

Tropical Fruit Sauce

Juice drained from 1 can (11-ounce-size) mandarin oranges

Juice drained from 1 can (8-ounce-size) crushed pineapple in juice

¹/₄ cup sugar

1 tablespoon cornstarch

¹/₄ teaspoon orange extract or pineapple extract

Combine fruit juices; pour 1 cup combined juice into medium saucepan and discard any remaining juices. Stir in sugar and cornstarch. Cook over medium heat, stirring constantly, until thickened. Remove from heat. Stir in orange extract or pineapple extract. Cool to room temperature before serving. Cover and refrigerate leftover sauce.

Makes about ³/₄ cup sauce

1st Birthday Cupcakes

1²/₃ **cups all-purpose flour**

1¹/₂ **cups sugar**

¹/₂ **cup HERSHEY'S Cocoa**

1¹/₂ **teaspoons baking soda**

1 **teaspoon salt**

¹/₂ **teaspoon baking powder**

2 **eggs**

¹/₂ **cup shortening**

1¹/₂ **cups buttermilk or sour milk***

1 **teaspoon vanilla extract**

ONE-BOWL BUTTERCREAM FROSTING (recipe follows)

To sour milk: Use 4¹/₂ teaspoons white vinegar plus milk to equal 1¹/₂ cups.

1. Heat oven to 350°F. Line muffin cups (2¹/₂ inches in diameter) with paper bake cups.

2. Stir together flour, sugar, cocoa, baking soda, salt and baking powder in large bowl. Add eggs, shortening, buttermilk and vanilla. Beat on low speed of mixer 1 minute, scraping bowl constantly. Beat on high speed 3 minutes, scraping bowl occasionally. Fill muffin cups ¹/₂ full with batter.

3. Bake 18 to 20 minutes or until wooden pick inserted in center comes out clean. Remove from pan to wire rack. Cool completely. Frost with ONE-BOWL BUTTERCREAM FROSTING.

HERSHEY'S® Chocolate Cake: Heat oven to 350°F. Grease two 9-inch round baking pans; line bottoms with wax paper. Prepare batter as directed above; pour into prepared pans. Bake 30 to 35 minutes or until wooden pick inserted in center comes out clean. Cool 10 minutes; remove from pans to wire racks. Remove paper. Cool completely. Frost with ONE-BOWL BUTTERCREAM FROSTING.

One-Bowl Buttercream Frosting

- **6 tablespoons butter or margarine, softened**
- **2²/₃ cups powdered sugar**
- **¹/₂ cup HERSHEY'S Cocoa**
- **¹/₃ cup milk**
- **1 teaspoon vanilla extract**

Beat butter in medium bowl. Add powdered sugar and cocoa alternately with milk and vanilla, beating to spreading consistency (additional milk may be needed).

Makes about 2 cups frosting

Toffee Topped Pineapple Upside-Down Cakes

¹/₄ **cup light corn syrup**

¹/₄ **cup (¹/₂ stick) butter or margarine, melted**

1 **cup HEATH BITS 'O BRICKLE Toffee Bits**

4 **pineapple rings**

4 **maraschino cherries**

¹/₄ **cup (¹/₂ stick) butter or margarine, softened**

²/₃ **cup sugar**

1 **egg**

1 **tablespoon rum or 1 teaspoon rum extract**

1¹/₃ **cups all-purpose flour**

2 **teaspoons baking powder**

²/₃ **cup milk**

1. Heat oven to 350°F. Lightly coat inside of 4 individual 2-cup baking dishes with vegetable oil spray.

2. Stir together 1 tablespoon corn syrup and 1 tablespoon melted butter in each of 4 baking dishes. Sprinkle each with ¹/₄ cup toffee. Center pineapple rings on toffee and place cherries in centers.

3. Beat softened butter and sugar in small bowl until blended. Add egg and rum, beating well. Stir together flour and baking powder; add alternately with milk to butter-sugar mixture, beating until smooth. Spoon about ³/₄ cup batter into each prepared dish.

4. Bake 25 to 30 minutes or until wooden pick inserted in center comes out clean. Immediately invert onto serving dishes; cool slightly before serving. Refrigerate leftovers.

Fudge Truffle Cheesecake

CHOCOLATE CRUMB CRUST (recipe follows)

2 cups (12-ounce package) HERSHEY'S SPECIAL DARK Chocolate Chips or HERSHEY'S Semi-Sweet Chocolate Chips

3 packages (8 ounces each) cream cheese, softened

1 can (14 ounces) sweetened condensed milk (not evaporated milk)

4 eggs

2 teaspoons vanilla extract

1. Prepare CHOCOLATE CRUMB CRUST; set aside. Heat oven to 300°F.

2. Place chocolate chips in microwave-safe bowl. Microwave at MEDIUM (50%) 1½ minutes; stir. If necessary, microwave at MEDIUM an additional 15 seconds at a time, stirring after each heating, just until chips are melted when stirred.

3. Beat cream cheese in large bowl until fluffy. Gradually beat in sweetened condensed milk until smooth. Add melted chips, eggs and vanilla; mix well. Pour into prepared crust.

4. Bake 1 hour and 5 minutes or until center is set. Remove from oven to wire rack. With knife, loosen cake from side of pan. Cool completely; remove side of pan. Refrigerate several hours before serving. Garnish as desired. Cover; refrigerate leftover cheesecake.

Chocolate Crumb Crust: Stir together 1½ cups vanilla wafer crumbs (about 45 cookies, crushed), ½ cup powdered sugar, ⅓ cup HERSHEY'S Cocoa and ⅓ cup melted butter or margarine in bowl. Press firmly onto bottom of 9-inch springform pan.

Chocolate Cherry Delight Cake

1 cup sugar

1 cup all-purpose flour

$^{1}/_{3}$ cup HERSHEY'S Cocoa

$^{3}/_{4}$ teaspoon baking soda

$^{3}/_{4}$ teaspoon baking powder

Dash salt

$^{1}/_{2}$ cup milk

2 eggs

$^{1}/_{4}$ cup vegetable oil

1 teaspoon vanilla extract

$^{1}/_{2}$ cup boiling water

1 container (8 ounces) frozen non-dairy whipped topping, thawed

1 can (21 ounces) cherry pie filling, chilled

1. Heat oven to 350°F. Line bottom of two 9-inch round pans with wax paper.

2. Combine sugar, flour, cocoa, baking soda, baking powder and salt in large bowl. Add milk, eggs, oil and vanilla; beat on medium speed of mixer 2 minutes. Stir in boiling water. (Batter will be thin.) Pour into prepared pans.

3. Bake 18 to 22 minutes or until wooden pick inserted in center comes out clean. Cool 10 minutes; remove from pans to wire racks. Carefully remove wax paper. Cool completely.

4. To assemble dessert, place one cake layer on serving plate. Spread with half of whipped topping; top with half of pie filling. Top with second cake layer. Spread with remaining topping and pie filling. Refrigerate at least 1 hour. Cover; refrigerate leftover cake.

Cakes & Cheesecakes

Ultra Chocolate Cheesecake

Makes 12 servings

MOCHA CRUMB CRUST
(recipe follows)

3 packages (8 ounces each) cream cheese, softened

1¼ cups sugar

1 container (8 ounces) dairy sour cream

2 teaspoons vanilla extract

½ cup HERSHEY'S Cocoa

2 tablespoons all-purpose flour

3 eggs

CHOCOLATE DRIZZLE
(recipe follows)

1. Prepare MOCHA CRUMB CRUST. Heat oven to 350°F.

2. Beat cream cheese and sugar in large bowl until fluffy. Add sour cream and vanilla; beat until blended. Add cocoa and flour; beat until blended. Add eggs; beat well. Pour into crust.

3. Bake 50 to 55 minutes or until set. Remove from oven to wire rack. With knife, loosen cake from side of pan. Cool completely; remove side of pan. Prepare CHOCOLATE DRIZZLE; drizzle over top. Refrigerate 4 to 6 hours. Cover; refrigerate leftover cheesecake.

Mocha Crumb Crust

1¼ cups vanilla wafer crumbs (about 40 wafers, crushed)

¼ cup sugar

¼ cup HERSHEY'S Cocoa

1 teaspoon powdered instant espresso or coffee

⅓ cup butter, melted

Heat oven to 350°F. Stir together crumbs, sugar, cocoa and instant espresso in medium bowl. Add butter; stir until well blended. Press mixture firmly onto bottom and 1 inch up side of 9-inch springform pan. Bake 8 minutes; cool slightly.

Chocolate Drizzle: Place ½ cup HERSHEY'S SPECIAL DARK Chocolate Chips or HERSHEY'S Semi-Sweet Chocolate Chips and 2 teaspoons shortening (do not use butter, margarine, spread or oil) in small microwave-safe bowl. Microwave at MEDIUM (50%) 30 seconds; stir. If necessary, microwave at MEDIUM an additional 10 seconds at a time, stirring after each heating, just until chips are melted and mixture is smooth.

Fiesta Fantasy Cake

2 cups sifted cake flour
  or 1³/₄ cups sifted
  all-purpose flour

¹/₂ cup HERSHEY'S SPECIAL
  DARK Cocoa or
  HERSHEY'S Cocoa

2 teaspoons baking soda

¹/₄ teaspoon salt

2 cups packed light brown
  sugar

²/₃ cup butter, softened

3 eggs

1 tablespoon coffee liqueur
  or strong coffee

¹/₂ teaspoon vanilla extract

1 container (8 ounces) dairy
  sour cream

³/₄ cup boiling water

CHOCOLATE MOUSSE
  (recipe follows)

CHOCOLATE FROSTING
  (recipe follows)

1. Heat oven to 350°F. Grease and flour two 9-inch round cake pans. Combine flour, cocoa, baking soda and salt. Set aside.

2. Beat brown sugar and butter with electric mixer on low or medium speed in large bowl until combined. Add eggs, one at a time, beating well after each addition. Beat in coffee liqueur or coffee and vanilla. Add flour mixture and sour cream alternately to sugar mixture, beating after each addition just until combined. Stir in boiling water until blended. Pour into prepared pans.

3. Bake 30 to 35 minutes or until wooden pick inserted near center comes out clean. Cool in pans on wire racks 10 minutes; remove from pans to wire racks. Cool completely.

4. Prepare CHOCOLATE MOUSSE. Split each cake layer horizontally to make four layers total. Place one layer on serving plate; spread with ¹/₃ (about 1 cup) CHOCOLATE MOUSSE. Repeat layering with two of the remaining layers and remaining mousse. Place remaining cake layer on top. Prepare CHOCOLATE FROSTING; frost cake top and sides. Cover; refrigerate at least 2 hours before serving.

Chocolate Mousse

2 cups (12-ounce package) HERSHEY'S SPECIAL DARK Chocolate Chips or HERSHEY'S Semi-Sweet Chocolate Chips

1¹⁄₃ cups whipping cream, divided

3 tablespoons granulated sugar

¹⁄₄ cup coffee liqueur or strong coffee

1 tablespoon vanilla extract

Place chocolate chips in food processor bowl; process until finely ground. Mix ¹⁄₃ cup whipping cream and granulated sugar in 1-quart saucepan. Cook over medium heat, stirring constantly, until sugar is dissolved and mixture is just boiling. With food processor running, pour hot cream through feed tube, processing 10 to 20 seconds or until chocolate is completely melted. Scrape side of food processor bowl. Add liqueur or strong coffee and vanilla; process 10 to 20 seconds or until smooth. Pour into large bowl; cool about 10 minutes or until mixture is room temperature. Beat remaining 1 cup whipping cream in chilled medium bowl with electric mixer on high speed just until soft peaks form. Fold whipped cream into chocolate mixture. Cover; refrigerate at least 30 minutes.

Makes about 3 cups mousse

Chocolate Frosting

1¹⁄₂ cups sifted powdered sugar

²⁄₃ cup HERSHEY'S SPECIAL DARK Cocoa

1¹⁄₂ cups whipping cream

1 teaspoon vanilla extract

3 to 4 tablespoons milk

Stir together powdered sugar and cocoa in medium mixer bowl. Stir in whipping cream and vanilla. Beat on low speed of mixer until stiff peaks form, scraping side of bowl constantly. (Mixture will be very stiff.) By hand, stir in milk 1 tablespoon at a time to make desired consistency.

Makes about 3 cups frosting

HERSHEY'S® Red Velvet Cake

¹/₂ **cup (1 stick) butter or margarine, softened**

1¹/₂ **cups sugar**

2 **eggs**

1 **teaspoon vanilla extract**

1 **cup buttermilk or sour milk***

2 **tablespoons (1-ounce bottle) red food color**

2 **cups all-purpose flour**

¹/₃ **cup HERSHEY'S Cocoa**

1 **teaspoon salt**

1¹/₂ **teaspoons baking soda**

1 **tablespoon white vinegar**

1 **to 2 cans (16 ounces each) ready-to-spread vanilla frosting**

HERSHEY'S Mini Chips Semi-Sweet Chocolate, HERSHEY'S Milk Chocolate Chips or red sugar sprinkles (optional)

To sour milk: Use 1 tablespoon white vinegar plus milk to equal 1 cup.

1. Heat oven to 350°F. Grease and flour 13×9×2-inch baking pan.**

2. Beat butter and sugar in large bowl; add eggs and vanilla, beating well. Stir together buttermilk and food color. Stir together flour, cocoa and salt; add alternately to butter mixture with buttermilk mixture, mixing well. Stir in baking soda and vinegar. Pour into prepared pan.

3. Bake 30 to 35 minutes or until wooden pick inserted in center comes out clean. Cool completely in pan on wire rack. Frost; garnish with chocolate chips or red sugar sprinkles, if desired.

**This recipe can be made in 2 (9-inch) cake pans. Bake at 350°F for 30 to 35 minutes or until wooden pick inserted in center comes out clean. Cool 10 minutes; remove from pans. Cool completely. Frost as directed.

For Heart Shapes: Using open-topped heart-shaped cookie cutter (at least 1¹/₂ inches deep and 3 inches wide), cut cake into 12 hearts. Frost and decorate as directed.

HERSHEY'S® Red Velvet Cupcakes: Line 28 muffin cups (2¹/₂ inches in diameter) with paper or foil bake cups. Prepare batter as above; fill each muffin cup about ¹/₂ full with batter. Bake at 350°F about 20 minutes or until wooden pick inserted in center comes out clean. Cool in pan on wire rack. Frost as directed. Makes 28 cupcakes.

Chocolate MINI KISSES® Truffle Cake

1¼ cups (2½ sticks) butter (no substitutions)

¾ cup HERSHEY'S SPECIAL DARK Cocoa or HERSHEY'S Cocoa

1 cup plus 1 tablespoon sugar, divided

1 tablespoon all-purpose flour

2 teaspoons vanilla extract

4 eggs, separated

1 cup HERSHEY'S MINI KISSESBRAND Milk Chocolates

1 tub (8 ounces) frozen whipped topping, thawed

2 teaspoons HERSHEY'S SPECIAL DARK Cocoa or HERSHEY'S Cocoa

1. Heat oven to 425°F. Grease bottom of 9-inch springform pan.

2. Melt butter in medium microwave-safe bowl; add ¾ cup cocoa and 1 cup sugar, stirring until well blended. Cool 5 minutes.

3. Stir in flour and vanilla; add egg yolks, beating well after each addition. Beat egg whites with remaining 1 tablespoon sugar in medium bowl until soft peaks form; gradually fold into chocolate mixture. Add chocolates. Spoon batter into prepared pan.

4. Bake 15 to 18 minutes or just until edges are firm (1-inch circle in center will be soft). With spatula, loosen cake from side of pan. Cool completely on wire rack; remove side of pan.

5. Cover; refrigerate at least 6 hours. Sift 2 teaspoons cocoa over whipped topping; stir until well blended. Garnish cake with chocolate topping. Cut cake while cold; garnish with additional chocolates.

German Chocolate Cheesecake

COCONUT-PECAN GRAHAM CRUST (recipe follows)

1 package (4 ounces) **HERSHEY'S Semi-Sweet Chocolate Baking Bar, broken into pieces**

3 packages (8 ounces each) **cream cheese, softened**

³/₄ **cup sugar**

¹/₂ **cup dairy sour cream**

2 teaspoons **vanilla extract**

2 tablespoons **all-purpose flour**

3 **eggs**

COCONUT-PECAN TOPPING (recipe follows)

1. Prepare COCONUT-PECAN GRAHAM CRUST. Increase oven temperature to 450°F.

2. Place chocolate in small microwave-safe bowl. Microwave at MEDIUM (50%) 1 to 1¹/₂ minutes or until chocolate is melted and smooth when stirred; set aside. Combine cream cheese, sugar, sour cream and vanilla in large bowl; beat on medium speed of mixer until smooth. Add flour, 1 tablespoon at a time, blending well. Add eggs and melted chocolate; blend well. Pour into prepared crust.

3. Bake 10 minutes; without opening oven door, reduce oven temperature to 250°F. Continue baking 35 minutes; remove from oven. With knife, loosen cake from side of pan. Cool completely; remove side of pan.

4. Prepare COCONUT-PECAN TOPPING; spread topping over top of cake. Refrigerate until firm before serving. Cover; refrigerate leftover cheesecake.

Coconut-Pecan Graham Crust

1 **cup graham cracker crumbs**

2 tablespoons **sugar**

¹/₃ **cup butter or margarine, melted**

¹/₄ **cup MOUNDS Sweetened Coconut Flakes**

¹/₄ **cup chopped pecans**

Heat oven to 350°F. Combine graham cracker crumbs and sugar in small bowl. Stir in butter, coconut and pecans. Press mixture onto bottom and ¹/₂ inch up side of 9-inch springform pan. Bake 8 to 10 minutes. Cool completely.

Coconut-Pecan Topping

- ¹/₂ **cup (1 stick) butter or margarine**
- ¹/₄ **cup packed light brown sugar**
- 2 **tablespoons light cream**
- 2 **tablespoons light corn syrup**
- 1 **cup MOUNDS Sweetened Coconut Flakes**
- ¹/₂ **cup chopped pecans**
- 1 **teaspoon vanilla extract**

Melt butter in small saucepan; add brown sugar, light cream and corn syrup. Cook over medium heat, stirring constantly, until smooth and bubbly. Remove from heat. Stir in coconut, pecans and vanilla. Cool slightly.

Microwave Directions: Place butter in microwave-safe bowl. Microwave at HIGH (100%) 30 seconds to 1 minute or until melted. Add brown sugar, light cream and corn syrup. Microwave at HIGH 2¹/₂ to 3 minutes, stirring every 30 seconds, until smooth. Stir in coconut, pecans and vanilla. Cool slightly.

Peppermint Pattie Cheesecake

CHOCOLATE CRUMB CRUST
(recipe follows)

3 **packages (8 ounces each)**
cream cheese, softened

¾ **cup sugar**

½ **cup dairy sour cream**

2 **teaspoons vanilla extract**

3 **tablespoons all-purpose**
flour

3 **eggs**

18 **small (1½-inch) YORK**
Peppermint Patties,
unwrapped and quartered

2 **tablespoons milk**

Whipped cream (optional)

1. Prepare CHOCOLATE CRUMB CRUST. Heat oven to 450°F.

2. Beat cream cheese, sugar, sour cream and vanilla in large bowl until smooth. Add flour, 1 tablespoon at a time, blending well. Add eggs; blend just until smooth. Place peppermint pattie pieces and milk in medium microwave-safe bowl. Microwave at MEDIUM (50%) 1 to 1½ minutes or just until candy is melted and smooth when stirred. Add to cream cheese mixture, blending until smooth. Pour into prepared crust.

3. Bake 10 minutes. Reduce oven temperature to 250°F; continue baking 40 to 45 minutes or until center appears set. Remove from oven to wire rack; with knife, loosen cake from side of pan. Cool completely; remove side of pan. Cover; refrigerate. Garnish with whipped cream, if desired. Cover; refrigerate leftovers.

Chocolate Crumb Crust: Place 6 tablespoons butter or margarine in medium microwave-safe bowl. Microwave at MEDIUM (50%) 30 seconds or until melted. Stir in 1½ cups finely crushed vanilla wafers (about 45 wafers, crushed), 6 tablespoons powdered sugar and 6 tablespoons HERSHEY'S Cocoa; blend well. Press mixture onto bottom and ½ to 1 inch up side of 9-inch springform pan.

Old-Fashioned Chocolate Cake

$3/4$ cup ($1^1/2$ sticks) butter or margarine, softened

$1^2/3$ cups sugar

3 eggs

1 teaspoon vanilla extract

2 cups all-purpose flour

$2/3$ cup HERSHEY'S Cocoa

$1^1/4$ teaspoons baking soda

1 teaspoon salt

$1/4$ teaspoon baking powder

$1^1/3$ cups water

$1/2$ cup finely crushed hard peppermint candy (optional)

ONE-BOWL BUTTERCREAM FROSTING (recipe follows)

Additional crushed hard peppermint candy (optional)

1. Heat oven to 350°F. Grease and flour two 9-inch round baking pans or one 13×9×2-inch baking pan.

2. Combine butter, sugar, eggs and vanilla in large bowl; beat on high speed of mixer 3 minutes. Stir together flour, cocoa, baking soda, salt and baking powder; add alternately with water to butter mixture. Blend just until combined; add candy, if desired. Pour batter into prepared pans.

3. Bake 30 to 35 minutes or until wooden pick inserted in center comes out clean. Cool 10 minutes; remove from pans to wire racks. Cool completely.

4. Frost with ONE-BOWL BUTTERCREAM FROSTING. Just before serving, garnish with peppermint candy, if desired.

One-Bowl Buttercream Frosting

6 tablespoons butter or margarine, softened

$2^2/3$ cups powdered sugar

$1/2$ cup HERSHEY'S Cocoa

$1/3$ cup milk

1 teaspoon vanilla extract

Beat butter in medium bowl. Add powdered sugar and cocoa alternately with milk, beating to spreading consistency (additional milk may be needed). Stir in vanilla.

Makes about 2 cups frosting

Chocolate Truffle Cake Supreme

1¼ cups (2½ sticks) unsalted butter

¾ cup HERSHEY'S Cocoa

1 cup plus 1 tablespoon sugar, divided

1 tablespoon all-purpose flour

2 teaspoons vanilla extract

4 eggs, separated

1 cup (½ pint) cold whipping cream

Chocolate curls (optional)

1. Heat oven to 425°F. Grease bottom of 8-inch springform pan.

2. Melt butter in medium saucepan over low heat. Add cocoa and 1 cup sugar; stir well. Remove from heat; cool slightly. Stir in flour and vanilla. Add egg yolks, one at a time, beating well after each addition.

3. Beat egg whites in medium bowl with remaining 1 tablespoon sugar until soft peaks form; gradually fold into chocolate mixture. Spoon batter into prepared pan.

4. Bake 16 to 18 minutes or until edge is firm (center will be soft). Cool completely on wire rack (cake will sink slightly in center as it cools). Remove side of pan. Refrigerate cake at least 6 hours.

5. Beat whipping cream in small bowl until soft peaks form; spread over top of cake. Cut cake while cold, but let stand at room temperature 10 to 15 minutes before serving. Garnish with chocolate curls, if desired.

REESE'S® Marble Cheesecake

**CRUMB CRUST (recipe
follows)**

**3 packages (8 ounces each)
cream cheese, softened**

1 cup sugar, divided

$^1/_2$ cup dairy sour cream

1 tablespoon vanilla extract

3 eggs

**3 tablespoons all-purpose
flour**

$^1/_4$ cup HERSHEY'S Cocoa

1 tablespoon vegetable oil

**$1^1/_3$ cups REESE'S Peanut Butter
Chips (reserved from
crust)**

$^1/_4$ cup milk

1. Heat oven to 450°F. Prepare
CRUMB CRUST.

2. Beat cream cheese, $^3/_4$ cup sugar,
sour cream and vanilla in large bowl
on medium speed of electric mixer
until smooth. Add eggs and flour;
beat until blended.

3. Beat cocoa, remaining $^1/_4$ cup
sugar and oil with $1^1/_2$ cups cheese
mixture in medium bowl. Place
$1^1/_3$ cups peanut butter chips and
milk in small microwave-safe bowl.
Microwave at MEDIUM (50%)
30 seconds; stir. If necessary,
microwave at MEDIUM an additional
15 seconds at a time, stirring after
each heating, until chips are melted
when stirred. Gradually add warm
peanut butter mixture to remaining
vanilla batter; beat on high speed
5 minutes.

4. Spoon peanut butter and
chocolate mixtures alternately over
prepared crust. Gently swirl with
knife or spatula for marbled effect.

5. Bake 10 minutes.* Without
opening oven door, decrease
temperature to 250°F and continue
to bake 30 minutes. Turn off oven;
leave cheesecake in oven 30 minutes
without opening door. Remove
from oven to wire rack; with knife,
loosen cake from side of pan. Cool
completely; remove side of pan.
Refrigerate until serving time. Cover;
refrigerate leftover cheesecake.

*Cheesecakes are less likely to crack if
baked in a water bath.*

Crumb Crust

1²/₃ cups (10-ounce package) REESE'S Peanut Butter Chips, divided

1¹/₄ cups vanilla wafer crumbs (about 40 wafers, crushed)

¹/₄ cup HERSHEY'S Cocoa

¹/₄ cup powdered sugar

¹/₄ cup (¹/₂ stick) butter or margarine, melted

With knife or food processor, chop ¹/₃ cup peanut butter chips (reserve remaining chips for cheesecake batter). Stir together crumbs, cocoa, powdered sugar and butter in medium bowl. Stir in chopped peanut butter chips. Press firmly onto bottom of 9-inch springform pan or 9-inch square pan.

Nutty Toffee Coffee Cake

1⅓ cups (8-ounce package) **HEATH BITS 'O BRICKLE Toffee Bits, divided**

⅓ cup plus ¾ cup packed **light brown sugar, divided**

2¼ cups all-purpose flour, **divided**

9 tablespoons butter or **margarine, softened and divided**

¾ cup granulated sugar

2 teaspoons baking powder

½ teaspoon ground cinnamon

¼ teaspoon salt

1¼ cups milk

1 egg

1 teaspoon vanilla extract

¾ cup chopped nuts

1. Heat oven to 350°F. Grease and flour 13×9×2-inch baking pan. Stir together ½ cup toffee bits, ⅓ cup brown sugar, ¼ cup flour and 3 tablespoons butter. Stir until crumbly; set aside.

2. Combine remaining 2 cups flour, granulated sugar, remaining ¾ cup brown sugar, remaining 6 tablespoons butter, baking powder, cinnamon and salt in large mixer bowl; mix until well blended. Gradually add milk, egg and vanilla, beating until thoroughly blended. Stir in remaining toffee bits and nuts. Spread batter in prepared pan.

3. Sprinkle reserved crumb topping over batter. Bake 30 to 35 minutes or until wooden pick inserted in center comes out clean. Serve warm or cool.

Chocolate Rum Pecan Pound Cake

$^2/_3$ **cup HERSHEY'S Cocoa, divided**

$^1/_4$ **cup boiling water**

$1^1/_4$ **cups (2$^1/_2$ sticks) butter or margarine, softened**

$2^2/_3$ **cups sugar**

1 **teaspoon vanilla extract**

5 **eggs**

2 **cups all-purpose flour**

1 **teaspoon salt**

$^1/_2$ **teaspoon baking powder**

$^1/_4$ **teaspoon baking soda**

$^1/_2$ **cup buttermilk or sour milk***

$^3/_4$ **cup finely chopped pecans**

$^1/_4$ **cup light rum or 1$^1/_2$ teaspoons rum extract plus $^1/_4$ cup water**

SATINY MINI CHIPS GLAZE (recipe follows)

Additional chopped pecans (optional)

***To sour milk:** Use 1$^1/_2$ teaspoons white vinegar plus milk to equal $^1/_2$ cup.*

1. Heat oven to 325°F. Grease and flour 12-cup fluted tube pan.

2. Stir $^1/_3$ cup cocoa and water in small bowl until smooth; set aside. Beat butter, sugar and vanilla in large bowl until fluffy. Add eggs, one at a time, beating well after each addition. Add reserved cocoa mixture; beat well. Stir together flour, remaining $^1/_3$ cup cocoa, salt, baking powder and baking soda; add to butter mixture alternately with buttermilk, beating well after each addition. Stir in pecans and rum. Pour batter into prepared pan.

3. Bake 1 hour and 5 minutes or until wooden pick inserted in center comes out clean. Cool 10 minutes; remove from pan to wire rack. Cool completely. Prepare SATINY MINI CHIPS GLAZE; drizzle over cake. Top with chopped pecans, if desired.

Satiny Mini Chips Glaze: Combine $^1/_4$ cup sugar and $^1/_4$ cup water in small saucepan. Cook over medium heat, stirring constantly, until sugar is dissolved and mixture begins to boil. Remove from heat; add 1 cup HERSHEY'S Mini Chips Semi-Sweet Chocolate, stirring until melted. Continue stirring until glaze is of desired consistency. Makes about 1 cup glaze.

Pies
&
Desserts

Chocolate Peanut Clusters

Makes about 2 dozen candies

¹/₂ **cup HERSHEY'S Milk Chocolate Chips**

¹/₂ **cup HERSHEY'S SPECIAL DARK Chocolate Chips or HERSHEY'S Semi-Sweet Chocolate Chips**

1 **tablespoon shortening (do not use butter, margarine, spread or oil)**

1 **cup unsalted, roasted peanuts**

1. Place milk chocolate chips, SPECIAL DARK chocolate chips and shortening in small microwave-safe bowl. Microwave at MEDIUM (50%) 1 to 1¹/₂ minutes or just until chips are melted and mixture is smooth when stirred. Stir in peanuts.

2. Drop by teaspoons into 1-inch diameter candy or petit four papers. Refrigerate until firm, about 1 hour. Store in airtight container in cool, dry place.

Chocolate Raspberry Dessert

1 cup all-purpose flour

1 cup sugar

$^1/_2$ cup (1 stick) butter or margarine, softened

$^1/_4$ teaspoon baking powder

4 eggs

$1^1/_2$ cups HERSHEY'S Syrup*

RASPBERRY CREAM CENTER (recipe follows)

CHOCOLATE GLAZE (recipe follows)

One 16-ounce can HERSHEY'S Syrup contains $1^1/_2$ cups syrup.

1. Heat oven to 350°F. Grease 13×9×2-inch baking pan.

2. Combine flour, sugar, butter, baking powder and eggs in large bowl; beat until smooth. Add syrup; blend thoroughly. Pour batter into prepared pan.

3. Bake 25 to 30 minutes or until wooden pick inserted in center comes out clean. Cool completely in pan on wire rack. Spread RASPBERRY CREAM CENTER on cake. Cover; refrigerate. Pour CHOCOLATE GLAZE over chilled dessert. Cover; refrigerate at least 1 hour before serving. Cover; refrigerate leftover dessert.

Raspberry Cream Center:
Combine 2 cups powdered sugar, $^1/_2$ cup (1 stick) softened butter or margarine and 2 tablespoons raspberry-flavored liqueur* in small bowl; beat until smooth. (A few drops red food coloring may be added, if desired.)

$^1/_4$ cup raspberry preserves mixed with 1 teaspoon water may be substituted for the raspberry-flavored liqueur.

Chocolate Glaze: Melt 6 tablespoons butter or margarine and 1 cup HERSHEY'S SPECIAL DARK Chocolate Chips or HERSHEY'S Semi-Sweet Chocolate Chips in small saucepan over very low heat. Remove from heat; stir until smooth. Cool slightly.

Peanut Butter Chip Brittle

1²/₃ **cups (10-ounce package) REESE'S Peanut Butter Chips, divided**

1¹/₂ **cups (3 sticks) butter or margarine**

1³/₄ **cups sugar**

3 **tablespoons light corn syrup**

3 **tablespoons water**

1. Butter 15¹/₂×10¹/₂×1-inch jelly-roll pan.* Sprinkle 1 cup peanut butter chips evenly onto bottom of prepared pan; set aside.

2. Melt butter in heavy 2¹/₂-quart saucepan; stir in sugar, corn syrup and water. Cook over medium heat, stirring constantly, until mixture reaches 300°F on candy thermometer. (This should take 30 to 35 minutes. Bulb of thermometer should not rest on bottom of saucepan.)

3. Remove from heat. Immediately spread mixture in prepared pan; sprinkle with remaining ²/₃ cup peanut butter chips. Cool completely. Remove from pan. Break into pieces. Store in tightly covered container in cool, dry place.

For thicker brittle, use a 13×9-inch pan.

Classic Chocolate Cream Pie

5 sections (¹/₂ ounce each) HERSHEY'S Unsweetened Chocolate Baking Bar, broken into pieces

3 cups milk, divided

1¹/₃ cups sugar

3 tablespoons all-purpose flour

3 tablespoons cornstarch

¹/₂ teaspoon salt

3 egg yolks

2 tablespoons butter or margarine

1¹/₂ teaspoons vanilla extract

1 baked (9-inch) pie crust, cooled, or 1 (9-inch) crumb crust

Sweetened whipped cream (optional)

1. Combine chocolate and 2 cups milk in medium saucepan; cook over medium heat, stirring constantly, just until mixture boils. Remove from heat and set aside.

2. Stir together sugar, flour, cornstarch and salt in medium bowl. Whisk remaining 1 cup milk into egg yolks in separate bowl; stir into sugar mixture. Gradually add to chocolate mixture. Cook over medium heat, whisking constantly, until mixture boils; boil and stir 1 minute. Remove from heat; stir in butter and vanilla.

3. Pour into prepared crust; press plastic wrap directly onto surface. Cool; refrigerate until well chilled. Top with whipped cream, if desired.

Chocolate Marbled Peanut Butter Pie

$^1/_2$ **cup REESE'S Creamy Peanut Butter**

1 **package (3 ounces) cream cheese, softened**

$^1/_2$ **teaspoon vanilla extract**

1 **cup powdered sugar**

$^1/_2$ **cup milk**

1 **container (8 ounces) frozen non-dairy whipped topping, thawed**

1 **extra serving-size packaged graham crumb crust (9 ounces)**

$^1/_2$ **cup HERSHEY'S SPECIAL DARK Chocolate Chips or HERSHEY'S Semi-Sweet Chocolate Chips**

1. Beat peanut butter, cream cheese and vanilla in medium bowl on medium speed of mixer until smooth. Gradually add powdered sugar and milk, beating until smooth. Fold in whipped topping. Place 1 cup peanut butter mixture in separate bowl. Spread remaining mixture in crust.

2. Place chocolate chips in small microwave-safe bowl. Microwave at MEDIUM (50%) 30 seconds or until chocolate is melted and smooth when stirred. Stir chocolate into reserved peanut butter mixture, blending thoroughly; drop by tablespoons onto top of pie. Using knife or spatula, gently swirl for marbled effect.

3. Cover; freeze 4 to 5 hours or until firm. Garnish as desired.

Classic Boston Cream Pie

1/3 cup shortening

1 cup sugar

2 eggs

1 teaspoon vanilla extract

1 1/4 cups all-purpose flour

1 1/2 teaspoons baking powder

1/4 teaspoon salt

3/4 cup milk

RICH FILLING (recipe follows)

DARK COCOA GLAZE (recipe follows)

1. Heat oven to 350°F. Grease and flour 9-inch round baking pan.

2. Beat shortening, sugar, eggs and vanilla in large bowl until fluffy. Stir together flour, baking powder and salt; add alternately with milk to shortening mixture, beating well after each addition. Pour batter into prepared pan.

3. Bake 30 to 35 minutes or until wooden pick inserted in center comes out clean. Cool 10 minutes; remove from pan to wire rack. Cool completely.

4. Prepare RICH FILLING. With long serrated knife, cut cake in half horizontally. Place one layer, cut side up, on serving plate; spread with prepared filling. Top with remaining layer, cut side down. Prepare DARK COCOA GLAZE; spread over cake, allowing glaze to run down sides. Refrigerate several hours or until cold. Garnish as desired. Refrigerate leftover dessert.

Rich Filling

1/3 cup sugar

2 tablespoons cornstarch

1 1/2 cups milk

2 egg yolks, slightly beaten

1 tablespoon butter or margarine

1 teaspoon vanilla extract

Stir together sugar and cornstarch in medium saucepan; gradually add milk and egg yolks, stirring until blended. Cook over medium heat, stirring constantly, until mixture comes to a boil. Boil 1 minute, stirring constantly. Remove from heat; stir in butter and vanilla. Cover; refrigerate several hours or until cold.

Makes about 1 1/3 cups filling

Dark Cocoa Glaze

- **3 tablespoons water**
- **2 tablespoons butter or margarine**
- **3 tablespoons HERSHEY'S Cocoa**
- **1 cup powdered sugar**
- **1/2 teaspoon vanilla extract**

Heat water and butter in small saucepan over medium heat until mixture comes to a boil; remove from heat. Immediately stir in cocoa. Gradually add powdered sugar and vanilla, beating with whisk until smooth and of desired consistency; cool slightly.

Makes about 3/4 cup glaze

Flourless Chocolate Torte

1¼ cups (2½ sticks) butter
¾ cup HERSHEY'S Cocoa
2 cups sugar, divided
6 eggs, separated
¼ cup water
1 teaspoon vanilla extract
1 cup blanched sliced almonds, toasted and ground*
½ cup plain dry bread crumbs
MOCHA CREAM (recipe follows)

*To toast almonds: Heat oven to 350°F. Place almonds in single layer in shallow baking pan. Bake 7 to 8 minutes, stirring occasionally, until light brown. Cool.

1. Heat oven to 350°F. Grease and flour 9-inch springform pan. Melt butter in saucepan over low heat. Add cocoa and 1½ cups sugar; stir until smooth. Cool to room temperature.

2. Beat egg yolks in large bowl until thick. Gradually beat in chocolate mixture; stir in water and vanilla. Combine ground almonds and bread crumbs; stir into chocolate mixture.

3. Beat egg whites until foamy; gradually add remaining ½ cup sugar, beating until soft peaks form. Fold about one-third of egg whites into chocolate. Fold chocolate into remaining egg whites. Pour into prepared pan.

4. Bake 50 to 60 minutes or until wooden pick inserted in center comes out clean. Cool 10 minutes. Loosen cake from side of pan; remove pan. Cool completely. Spread MOCHA CREAM over top. Sift with cocoa just before serving. Store covered in refrigerator.

Mocha Cream: Combine 1 cup (½ pint) cold whipping cream, 2 tablespoons powdered sugar, 1½ teaspoons powdered instant coffee dissolved in 1 teaspoon water and ½ teaspoon vanilla extract in medium bowl; beat until stiff. Makes about 2 cups.

Pies & Desserts

118

Chocolate Pecan Pie

1 cup sugar

1/3 cup HERSHEY'S Cocoa

3 eggs, lightly beaten

3/4 cup light corn syrup

1 tablespoon butter or margarine, melted

1 teaspoon vanilla extract

1 cup pecan halves

1 unbaked (9-inch) pie crust

Whipped topping (optional)

1. Heat oven to 350°F.

2. Stir together sugar and cocoa in medium bowl. Add eggs, corn syrup, butter and vanilla; stir until well blended. Stir in pecans. Pour into unbaked pie crust.

3. Bake 60 minutes or until set. Remove to wire rack and cool completely. Garnish with whipped topping, if desired.

Apple Toffee Crisp

Makes 10 to 12 servings

5 **cups (about 5 medium apples) peeled and sliced Granny Smith apples**

5 **cups (about 5 medium apples) peeled and sliced McIntosh apples**

1¼ **cups sugar, divided**

1¼ **cups all-purpose flour, divided**

¾ **cup (1½ sticks) butter or margarine, divided**

1⅓ **cups (8-ounce package) HEATH BITS 'O BRICKLE Toffee Bits**

1 **cup uncooked rolled oats**

½ **teaspoon ground cinnamon**

¼ **teaspoon baking powder**

¼ **teaspoon baking soda**

¼ **teaspoon salt**

Whipped topping or ice cream (optional)

1. Heat oven to 375°F. Grease 13×9×2-inch baking pan.

2. Toss apple slices, ¾ cup sugar and ¼ cup flour, coating apples evenly. Spread in bottom of prepared pan. Dot with ¼ cup (½ stick) butter.

3. Stir together toffee bits, oats, remaining ½ cup sugar, remaining 1 cup flour, cinnamon, baking powder, baking soda and salt. Melt remaining ½ cup (1 stick) butter; add to oat mixture, mixing until crumbs are formed. Sprinkle crumb mixture over apples.

4. Bake 45 to 50 minutes or until topping is lightly browned and apples are tender. Serve warm with whipped topping or ice cream, if desired. Cover; refrigerate leftovers.

Fudgey Mocha Nut Pie

6 **tablespoons butter or margarine**

¹/₃ **cup HERSHEY'S Cocoa**

1 **can (14 ounces) sweetened condensed milk (not evaporated milk)**

¹/₃ **cup water**

2 **eggs, beaten**

2 **to 3 tablespoons powdered instant coffee**

1 **cup HERSHEY'S SPECIAL DARK Chocolate Chips or HERSHEY'S Semi-Sweet Chocolate Chips**

1 **cup coarsely chopped pecans**

1 **teaspoon vanilla extract**

1 **unbaked (9-inch) pie crust**

Sweetened whipped cream (optional)

1. Heat oven to 350°F.

2. Melt butter in medium saucepan over low heat. Add cocoa; stir until smooth. Stir in sweetened condensed milk, water, eggs, instant coffee and chocolate chips; whisk constantly until well blended and chocolate is melted. Remove from heat.

3. Stir in pecans and vanilla. Pour into unbaked pie crust.

4. Bake 40 minutes or until center is set. (Center will still appear moist.) Cool completely. Garnish with sweetened whipped cream, if desired. Cover; refrigerate leftover pie.

Chocolate Strawberry Fruit Tart

1$^1/_3$ cups all-purpose flour

$^1/_2$ cup powdered sugar

$^1/_4$ cup HERSHEY'S Cocoa or HERSHEY'S SPECIAL DARK Cocoa

$^3/_4$ cup (1$^1/_2$ sticks) butter or margarine, softened

STRAWBERRY VANILLA FILLING (recipe follows)

$^1/_2$ cup HERSHEY'S SPECIAL DARK Chocolate Chips or HERSHEY'S Semi-Sweet Chocolate Chips

1 tablespoon shortening (do not use butter, margarine, spread or oil)

GLAZED FRUIT TOPPING (recipe follows)

Fresh fruit, sliced

1. Heat oven to 325°F. Grease and flour 12-inch pizza pan.

2. Stir together flour, powdered sugar and cocoa in medium bowl. With pastry blender, cut in butter until mixture holds together; press into prepared pan.

3. Bake 10 to 15 minutes or until crust is set. Cool completely.

4. Prepare STRAWBERRY VANILLA FILLING; spread over crust to within 1 inch of edge; refrigerate until filling is firm.

5. Place chocolate chips and shortening in small microwave-safe bowl. Microwave at MEDIUM (50%) 30 seconds; stir. If necessary, microwave at MEDIUM an additional 15 seconds at a time, stirring after each heating, just until chips are melted when stirred. Spoon chocolate into disposable pastry bag or corner of heavy duty plastic bag; cut off small piece at corner. Squeeze chocolate onto outer edge of filling in decorative design; refrigerate until chocolate is firm.

6. Prepare GLAZED FRUIT TOPPING. Arrange fresh fruit over filling; carefully brush prepared topping over fruit. Refrigerate until ready to serve. Cover; refrigerate leftover tart.

Strawberry Vanilla Filling

- **2 cups (12-ounce package) HERSHEY'S Premier White Chips**
- **¹/₄ cup evaporated milk**
- **1 package (8 ounces) cream cheese, softened**
- **1 teaspoon strawberry extract**
- **2 drops red food color**

1. Place white chips and evaporated milk in medium microwave-safe bowl. Microwave at MEDIUM (50%) 1 minute; stir. If necessary, microwave at MEDIUM an additional 15 seconds at a time, stirring after each heating, just until chips are melted when stirred.

2. Beat in cream cheese, strawberry extract and red food color.

Glazed Fruit Topping

- **¹/₄ teaspoon unflavored gelatin**
- **1 teaspoon cold water**
- **1¹/₂ teaspoons cornstarch or arrowroot**
- **¹/₄ cup apricot nectar or orange juice**
- **2 tablespoons sugar**
- **¹/₂ teaspoon lemon juice**

1. Sprinkle gelatin over water in small cup; let stand 2 minutes to soften.

2. Stir together cornstarch, apricot nectar, sugar and lemon juice in small saucepan. Cook over medium heat, stirring constantly, until mixture is thickened. Remove from heat; immediately stir in gelatin until smooth. Cool slightly.

Pies & Desserts

Chocolate Syrup Swirl Dessert

CRUMB CRUST (recipe
follows)

1 envelope unflavored gelatin

$1/4$ cup cold water

1 package (8 ounces) cream
cheese, softened

$1/4$ cup sugar

1 teaspoon vanilla extract

$3/4$ cup HERSHEY'S Syrup,
chilled

$3/4$ cup milk

VANILLA FILLING (recipe
follows)

Additional HERSHEY'S
Syrup (optional)

1. Prepare CRUMB CRUST.

2. Sprinkle gelatin over water in
small saucepan; let stand 2 minutes.
Cook over low heat, stirring
constantly, until gelatin is dissolved.

3. Beat cream cheese, sugar and
vanilla in large bowl until creamy.
Add syrup, gelatin mixture and
milk; blend well. Refrigerate, stirring
occasionally, until mixture mounds
from spoon, about 20 minutes.

4. Spoon one-half chocolate mixture
into prepared crust; top with one-
half VANILLA FILLING. Repeat
procedure, ending with spoonfuls

of VANILLA FILLING on top. Using
knife or metal spatula, gently swirl
through dessert. Cover; refrigerate
several hours until set. Serve with
additional syrup, if desired.

Crumb Crust: Stir together 2 cups
vanilla wafer crumbs (about 60
wafers, crushed) and $1/3$ cup melted
butter or margarine in medium bowl.
Press mixture onto bottom and
$1^1/2$ inches up side of 9-inch
springform pan or 10-inch pie plate.
Refrigerate about 30 minutes or until
firm.

Vanilla Filling

1 teaspoon unflavored gelatin

1 tablespoon cold water

2 tablespoons boiling water

1 cup ($1/2$ pint) cold whipping
cream

2 tablespoons sugar

$1/2$ teaspoon vanilla extract

Sprinkle gelatin over cold water in
small cup; let stand 1 minute. Add
boiling water; stir until gelatin is
completely dissolved; cool slightly.
Combine whipping cream, sugar and
vanilla in medium bowl; beat until
slightly thickened. Gradually add
gelatin mixture; beat until stiff.

Fresh Apple and Toffee Tart

4 to 6 large tart apples such as Granny Smith

¼ cup granulated sugar

2 tablespoons cornstarch or all-purpose flour

½ teaspoon ground cinnamon

1 package (15-ounce box) refrigerated pie crusts, softened as directed on box

1⅓ cups (8-ounce package) HEATH BITS 'O BRICKLE Toffee Bits, divided

2 teaspoons white decorator sugar crystals or granulated sugar, divided

Sweetened whipped cream or ice cream (optional)

1. Heat oven to 400°F. Peel and slice apples into thin slices. Toss apples with granulated sugar, cornstarch and cinnamon.

2. Unroll crusts; place each on ungreased cookie sheet. Sprinkle ⅓ cup toffee bits over each crust; press lightly into crust.

3. Starting 2 inches from the edge of the crust, arrange apple slices by overlapping slightly in a circular spiral toward the center of the crust. Sprinkle ⅓ cup of remaining toffee bits over each apple center. Fold 2-inch edge of crust over apples. Sprinkle each crust edge with 1 teaspoon sugar crystals.

4. Bake 25 to 30 minutes or until crust is golden. Cool slightly. Serve warm or cool with sweetened whipped cream or ice cream, if desired.

Note: Recipe may be halved.

HUGS® & KISSES® Crescents

1 package (8 ounces)
   refrigerated crescent
   dinner rolls

24 HERSHEY'S KISSESBRAND Milk
   Chocolates or HERSHEY'S
   HUGSBRAND Candies

   Powdered sugar

1. Heat oven to 375°F. Separate dough into 8 triangles. Remove wrappers from chocolates.

2. Place 2 chocolates at center of wide end of each triangle; place an additional chocolate on top of other two pieces. Starting at wide end, roll to opposite point; pinch edges to seal. Place rolls, pointed side down, on ungreased cookie sheet. Curve into crescent shape.

3. Bake 10 minutes or until lightly browned. Cool slightly; sift with powdered sugar. Serve warm.

Note: Leftover crescents can be reheated in microwave for a few seconds.

Chocolate Dream Cups

1 cup HERSHEY'S SPECIAL DARK Chocolate Chips or HERSHEY'S Semi-Sweet Chocolate Chips

1 teaspoon shortening (do not use butter, margarine, spread or oil)

CHOCOLATE FILLING or RASPBERRY FILLING (recipes follow)

1. Line 6 muffin cups (2$^1/_2$ inches in diameter) with paper bake cups.

2. Place chocolate chips and shortening in small microwave-safe bowl. Microwave at MEDIUM (50%) 1 minute; stir. If necessary, microwave at MEDIUM an additional 30 seconds or until chips are melted and mixture is smooth when stirred.

3. Coat inside pleated surface and bottoms of bake cups thickly and evenly with melted chocolate using a soft-bristled pastry brush. Refrigerate coated cups 10 minutes or until set; recoat any thin spots with melted chocolate. (If necessary, chocolate can be reheated on MEDIUM a few seconds.) Refrigerate cups until very firm, 2 hours or overnight. Carefully peel paper from each chocolate cup. Cover; refrigerate until ready to use.

4. Prepare either CHOCOLATE or RASPBERRY FILLING. Spoon or pipe into chocolate cups; refrigerate until set. Garnish as desired.

Chocolate Filling

1 teaspoon unflavored gelatin

1 tablespoon cold water

2 tablespoons boiling water

$^1/_2$ cup sugar

$^1/_4$ cup HERSHEY'S Cocoa

1 cup ($^1/_2$ pint) cold whipping cream

1 teaspoon vanilla extract

1. Sprinkle gelatin over cold water in small bowl; let stand 1 minute to soften. Add boiling water; stir until gelatin is completely dissolved and mixture is clear. Cool slightly.

2. Stir together sugar and cocoa in another small bowl; add whipping cream and vanilla. Beat on medium speed, scraping bottom of bowl occasionally until stiff. Pour in gelatin mixture; beat until well blended.

Raspberry Filling

- 1 **package (10 ounces) frozen red raspberries, thawed**
- 1 **teaspoon unflavored gelatin**
- 1 **tablespoon cold water**
- 2 **tablespoons boiling water**
- 1 **cup (¹/₂ pint) cold whipping cream**
- ¹/₄ **cup powdered sugar**
- ¹/₂ **teaspoon vanilla extract**
- 3 **to 4 drops red food color**

1. Drain raspberries; press berries through sieve to remove seeds. Discard seeds.

2. Sprinkle gelatin over cold water in small bowl; let stand 1 minute to soften. Add boiling water; stir until gelatin is completely dissolved and mixture is clear. Cool slightly.

3. Beat whipping cream, sugar and vanilla in another small bowl until soft peaks form; pour in gelatin mixture and beat until stiff. Carefully fold in raspberry purée and food color; refrigerate 20 minutes.

Mocha Brownie Nut Torte

1 cup (2 sticks) butter

1 package (4 ounces) HERSHEY'S Unsweetened Chocolate Baking Bar, broken into pieces

4 eggs

1 teaspoon vanilla extract

2 cups granulated sugar

1 cup all-purpose flour

1 cup finely chopped pecans

1 package (8 ounces) cream cheese, softened

1 cup powdered sugar

$1/2$ cup chilled whipping cream

2 to 3 teaspoons powdered instant coffee

CHOCOLATE GLAZE (recipe follows)

1. Heat oven to 350°F. Line bottom and sides of 9-inch round cake pan with foil, extending foil beyond sides. Grease foil.

2. Place butter and chocolate in medium microwave-safe bowl. Microwave at MEDIUM (50%) 1 minute; stir. If necessary, microwave an additional 15 seconds at a time, stirring after each heating, until chocolate is melted when stirred. Cool 5 minutes.

3. Beat eggs and vanilla in large bowl until foamy. Gradually beat in granulated sugar. Blend in chocolate mixture; fold in flour and pecans. Spread mixture in prepared pan. Bake 40 to 45 minutes or until wooden pick inserted in center comes out clean. Cool completely in pan on wire rack.

4. Use foil to lift brownie from pan; remove foil. Place brownie layer on serving plate. Beat cream cheese and powdered sugar in medium bowl until well blended. Beat whipping cream and instant coffee until stiff; gradually fold into cream cheese mixture, blending well. Spread over brownie layer. Cover; refrigerate until serving time.

5. Just before serving, prepare CHOCOLATE GLAZE. Drizzle generous tablespoon glaze over top and down sides of each serving.

Chocolate Glaze: Place 6 ounces ($1^1/2$ 4-ounce packages) HERSHEY'S Semi-Sweet Chocolate Baking Bar and $1/2$ cup whipping cream in small microwave-safe bowl. Microwave at MEDIUM (50%) 30 to 45 seconds or until chocolate is melted and mixture is smooth when stirred. Cool slightly. Makes 1 cup glaze.

Viennese Chocolate Torte

- ¹/₄ cup HERSHEY'S Cocoa
- ¹/₄ cup boiling water
- ¹/₃ cup shortening
- ³/₄ cup sugar
- ¹/₂ teaspoon vanilla extract
- 1 egg
- 1 cup all-purpose flour
- ³/₄ teaspoon baking soda
- ¹/₄ teaspoon salt
- ²/₃ cup buttermilk or sour milk*
- ¹/₄ cup seedless black raspberry preserves
- CREAM FILLING (recipe follows)
- COCOA GLAZE (recipe follows)
- MOUNDS Sweetened Coconut Flakes, toasted**

To sour milk: Use 2 teaspoons white vinegar plus milk to equal ²/₃ cup.

**To toast coconut:* Heat oven to 350°F. Spread coconut in even layer on baking sheet. Bake 6 to 8 minutes, stirring occasionally, until golden.

1. Heat oven to 350°F. Lightly grease 15¹/₂×10¹/₂×1-inch jelly-roll pan; line pan with wax paper and lightly grease paper.

2. Stir together cocoa and boiling water in small bowl until smooth; set aside. Beat shortening, sugar and vanilla in medium bowl until creamy; beat in egg. Stir together flour, baking soda and salt; add alternately with buttermilk to shortening mixture. Add reserved cocoa mixture, beating just until blended. Spread batter in pan.

3. Bake 16 to 18 minutes or until wooden pick inserted in center comes out clean. Cool 10 minutes; remove from pan. Remove wax paper; cool completely. Cut cake crosswise into three equal pieces. Place one piece on serving plate. Stir raspberry preserves to soften; spread 2 tablespoons evenly on top of cake. Spread half of CREAM FILLING over preserves. Repeat layering. Glaze top of torte with COCOA GLAZE, allowing some to drizzle down sides. Garnish with coconut. Refrigerate several hours. Cover; refrigerate leftover torte.

Cream Filling: Beat 1 cup (¹/₂ pint) whipping cream, 2 tablespoons powdered sugar and 1 teaspoon vanilla extract in small bowl until stiff. Makes about 2 cups filling.

Cocoa Glaze

- **2 tablespoons butter or margarine**
- **2 tablespoons HERSHEY'S Cocoa**
- **2 tablespoons water**
- **1 cup powdered sugar**
- **¹/₂ teaspoon vanilla extract**

Melt butter in saucepan over low heat. Stir in cocoa and water. Cook, stirring constantly, until mixture thickens. Do not boil. Remove from heat. Whisk in powdered sugar gradually. Add vanilla and beat with whisk until smooth. Add additional water, ¹/₂ teaspoon at a time, until desired consistency.

Makes about ³/₄ cup glaze.

Chocolate & Vanilla Swirl Tart

TART SHELL (recipe follows)

²/₃ cup **HERSHEY'S SPECIAL DARK Chocolate Chips or HERSHEY'S Semi-Sweet Chocolate Chips**

¹/₂ cup **milk, divided**

2 **tablespoons sugar**

¹/₂ **teaspoon unflavored gelatin**

1 **tablespoon cold water**

²/₃ cup **HERSHEY'S Premier White Chips**

1 **teaspoon vanilla extract**

1 cup (¹/₂ pint) **cold whipping cream**

1. Prepare TART SHELL.

2. Place chocolate chips, ¹/₄ cup milk and sugar in small microwave-safe bowl. Microwave at MEDIUM (50%) 1 minute; stir. If necessary, microwave at MEDIUM an additional 15 seconds at a time, stirring after each heating, just until chips are melted when stirred. Cool to room temperature (about 20 minutes).

3. Sprinkle gelatin over water in small cup; let stand 2 minutes to soften. Place white chips and remaining ¹/₄ cup milk in second small microwave-safe bowl. Microwave at MEDIUM 1 minute; stir. Add gelatin mixture and vanilla; stir until gelatin is dissolved. Cool to room temperature (about 20 minutes).

4. Beat whipping cream in small bowl on high speed of mixer until stiff; fold 1 cup whipped cream into vanilla mixture. Fold remaining whipped cream into chocolate mixture. Alternately, spoon chocolate and vanilla mixtures into prepared tart shell; swirl with knife for marbled effect. Refrigerate until firm. Cover; refrigerate leftover tart.

Tart Shell

- **¹/₂ cup (1 stick) butter (do not use margarine), softened**
- **2 tablespoons sugar**
- **2 egg yolks**
- **1 cup all-purpose flour**

1. Heat oven to 375°F. Grease bottom and sides of fluted 8- or 9-inch tart pan.

2. Beat butter and sugar in small bowl until blended. Add egg yolks; mix well. Stir in flour until mixture is crumbly. Press onto bottom and up sides of prepared pan. (If dough is sticky, sprinkle with 1 tablespoon flour.) Prick bottom with fork to prevent puffing.

3. Bake 8 to 10 minutes or until lightly browned. Cool completely.

Lighter Than Air Chocolate Delight

2 **envelopes unflavored gelatin**

¹/₂ **cup cold water**

1 **cup boiling water**

1¹/₃ **cups nonfat dry milk powder**

¹/₃ **cup HERSHEY'S SPECIAL DARK Cocoa or HERSHEY'S Cocoa**

1 **tablespoon vanilla extract**

Dash salt

Granulated sugar substitute to equal 14 teaspoons sugar

8 **large ice cubes**

1. Sprinkle gelatin over cold water in blender container; let stand 4 minutes to soften. Gently stir with rubber spatula, scraping gelatin particles off sides; add boiling water to gelatin mixture. Cover; blend until gelatin dissolves. Add milk powder, cocoa, vanilla and salt; blend on medium speed until well mixed. Add sugar substitute and ice cubes; blend on high speed until ice is crushed and mixture is smooth and fluffy.

2. Immediately pour into 4-cup mold. Cover; refrigerate until firm. Unmold onto serving plate.

Note: Eight individual dessert dishes may be used in place of 4-cup mold, if desired.

Toffee Crème Brûlée

Makes 6 to 9 desserts

1$\frac{1}{3}$ **cups (8-ounce package) HEATH BITS 'O BRICKLE Toffee Bits, divided**

1 **tablespoon plus $\frac{1}{4}$ cup sugar, divided**

1 **quart heavy cream**

Dash salt

7 **egg yolks**

1 **teaspoon vanilla extract**

1. Heat oven to 325°F. Place 6 to 7 (8-ounce) or 8 to 9 (6-ounce) ramekins or custard cups in baking pan with 2-inch sides. Crush $\frac{1}{4}$ cup toffee bits; combine with 1 tablespoon sugar. Set aside.

2. Place cream, remaining toffee bits, remaining $\frac{1}{4}$ cup sugar and salt in medium heavy saucepan. Heat over medium heat, stirring constantly, until cream is hot and toffee bits have melted.* Do not boil. Set aside.

3. Beat egg yolks with electric mixer in medium mixer bowl until light yellow. Gradually blend about half of the cream mixture into eggs. Gradually return egg/cream mixture to remaining cream mixture, blending well. Stir in vanilla. Divide mixture evenly into prepared cups. Add water to pan until it is halfway up the sides of cups.

4. Bake 40 to 45 minutes or until center is set, but still soft. (Custard will continue to cook after removal from oven.) Carefully remove cups from water; place on wire rack or allow cups to cool in pan on wire rack. Cool to room temperature. Loosely cover and refrigerate at least 2 hours. Allow crème brûlèe to stand at room temperature at least 20 minutes before serving.

5. Divide reserved toffee bits mixture in thin even layer over top of each cup. Heat toffee layer with propane torch or place under broiler of oven (2 to 3 minutes) until toffee is melting and surface is lightly browned, but does not burn. Allow to cool several minutes before serving. Garnish as desired.

Toffee will melt and small bits of almonds will remain. These will sink to bottom of dessert. Mixture can be strained to remove these bits, if desired.

Creme de Cacao Torte

2/3 cup butter or margarine, softened

1 2/3 cups sugar

3 eggs

1/2 teaspoon vanilla extract

2 cups all-purpose flour

2/3 cup HERSHEY'S Cocoa

1 1/4 teaspoons baking soda

1/4 teaspoon baking powder

1 1/3 cups milk

2 tablespoons creme de cacao (chocolate-flavored liqueur) (optional)

CREME DE CACAO FILLING (recipe follows)

CHOCOLATE GANACHE GLAZE (recipe follows)

1. Heat oven to 350°F. Grease and flour two 9-inch round baking pans.

2. Beat butter, sugar, eggs and vanilla in large bowl until blended. Stir together flour, cocoa, baking soda and baking powder; add to butter mixture alternately with milk, blending just until combined. Pour batter into prepared pans.

3. Bake 30 to 35 minutes or until wooden pick inserted in center comes out clean. Cool 10 minutes; remove from pans to wire racks. Sprinkle each layer with 1 tablespoon creme de cacao; cool completely.

4. Meanwhile, prepare CREME DE CACAO FILLING. Split each cake layer horizontally into 2 layers. Place one layer on serving plate; spread with one-third of FILLING. Repeat layering with remaining cake and FILLING, ending with cake layer. Cover tightly; refrigerate at least 8 hours.

5. Prepare CHOCOLATE GANACHE GLAZE; spoon on top of chilled cake, allowing GLAZE to drizzle down side of cake. Refrigerate.

Creme de Cacao Filling: Beat 1 cup (1/2 pint) cold whipping cream, 2 tablespoons creme de cacao (optional) and 1 tablespoon HERSHEY'S Cocoa in small bowl until stiff. Cover; refrigerate. Makes about 2 cups filling.

Chocolate Ganache Glaze

- **1 HERSHEY'S SPECIAL DARK Chocolate Bar (6.8 ounces), broken into pieces**
- **¼ cup whipping cream**
- **1 tablespoon butter**
- **1½ teaspoons creme de cacao (chocolate-flavored liqueur) or water**

Combine chocolate bar pieces, whipping cream and butter in medium saucepan; cook over low heat, stirring constantly, until chocolate is melted and mixture is smooth. Stir in creme de cacao. Cool to lukewarm (glaze will be slightly thickened).

Makes about 1 cup glaze

Easy Chocolate Mousse-Filled Tulip Cups

24 **wonton wrappers (refrigerated in produce department)**

2 **tablespoons butter or margarine, melted**

3 **tablespoons sugar, divided**

EASY CHOCOLATE MOUSSE (recipe follows)

1. Heat oven to 300°F.

2. Place individual wonton wrappers on wax paper; brush one side with butter. Sprinkle each wrapper evenly with scant $1/2$ teaspoonful sugar; press each wrapper, sugared side up, into ungreased small muffin cups ($1^3/_4$ inches in diameter) to form flower shape.

3. Bake 15 to 20 minutes or just until crisp and golden brown. Cool completely in pan on wire rack. Pipe or spoon EASY CHOCOLATE MOUSSE into center of each "tulip" cup. Cover; refrigerate. Refrigerate leftover cups.

Easy Chocolate Mousse: Beat 1 cup ($1/2$ pint) cold whipping cream, $1/2$ cup powdered sugar, $1/4$ cup HERSHEY'S Cocoa or HERSHEY'S SPECIAL DARK Cocoa and 1 teaspoon vanilla extract in medium bowl until stiff. Use immediately.

Peanut Butter Fondue

Makes about 3 cups fondue

Selection of fruits and other fondue dippers

3¹/₃ cups (two 10-ounce packages) REESE'S Peanut Butter Chips

1¹/₂ cups light cream

1. Prepare ahead of time a selection of fresh fruit chunks for dipping: apples, bananas, pears, peaches, cherries, pineapple, oranges (brush fresh fruit with lemon juice to prevent browning). Cover; refrigerate until ready to serve. (Dried apples and apricots, marshmallows and bite-size pieces of pound cake can also be used for dipping.)

2. Place peanut butter chips and light cream in medium microwave-safe bowl. Microwave at MEDIUM (50%) 1¹/₂ minutes; stir. If necessary, microwave at MEDIUM an additional 30 seconds at a time, stirring after each heating, until chips are melted and mixture is smooth when stirred.

3. Pour into fondue pot; keep warm over low heat. Dip chunks of fruit into warm sauce with forks. Keep leftover sauce covered and refrigerated.

Note: Recipe may be halved using 1 package (10 ounces) REESE'S Peanut Butter Chips and ³/₄ cup light cream.

Crispy Chocolate Ice Cream Mud Pie

Makes 8 servings

¹/₂ **cup HERSHEY'S Syrup**

¹/₃ **cup HERSHEY'S SPECIAL DARK Chocolate Chips or HERSHEY'S Semi-Sweet Chocolate Chips**

2 **cups crisp rice cereal**

4 **cups (1 quart) vanilla ice cream, divided**

4 **cups (1 quart) chocolate ice cream, divided**

Additional HERSHEY'S Syrup

1. Butter 9-inch pie plate.

2. Place ¹/₂ cup chocolate syrup and chocolate chips in medium microwave-safe bowl. Microwave at MEDIUM (50%) 45 seconds or until hot; stir until smooth. Reserve ¹/₄ cup chocolate syrup mixture; set aside. Add cereal to remaining chocolate syrup mixture, stirring until well coated; cool slightly.

3. Press cereal mixture, using back of spoon, evenly on bottom and up side of prepared pie plate to form crust. Place in freezer 15 to 20 minutes or until crust is firm. Spread half of vanilla ice cream into crust; spoon reserved ¹/₄ cup chocolate syrup mixture over layer. Spread half of chocolate ice cream over sauce.

4. Top with alternating scoops of vanilla and chocolate ice cream. Cover; return to freezer until serving time. Drizzle with additional chocolate syrup just before serving.

Chocolate Fried Ice Cream

1 **quart vanilla ice cream**

1 **cup vanilla wafer crumbs (about 30 wafers, crushed)**

$^1/_2$ **cup finely chopped pecans**

$^1/_2$ **cup MOUNDS Sweetened Coconut Flakes**

3 **tablespoons HERSHEY'S Cocoa**

2 **eggs**

Vegetable oil

CHOCOLATE NUT SAUCE (recipe follows)

1. Cover tray with wax paper. Form 6 ice cream balls with scoop; place on prepared tray. Cover; freeze several hours or until very firm.

2. Stir together vanilla wafer crumbs, nuts, coconut and cocoa in medium bowl; set aside. Beat eggs in small bowl. Coat ice cream balls with crumb mixture, pressing crumbs firmly into ice cream. Dip balls in beaten egg; coat again with crumb mixture. Place on prepared tray; freeze 2 hours or until very firm.

3. Just before serving, heat 2 inches oil in fry pan or deep fryer to 375°F. Remove 2 balls at a time from freezer; fry in hot oil 20 to 25 seconds or until browned. Drain; serve immediately with CHOCOLATE NUT SAUCE.

Chocolate Nut Sauce

3 **tablespoons butter or margarine**

$^1/_3$ **cup pecan pieces**

$^2/_3$ **cup sugar**

$^1/_4$ **cup HERSHEY'S Cocoa**

$^1/_8$ **teaspoon salt**

$^1/_2$ **cup light cream**

$^1/_2$ **teaspoon vanilla extract**

1. Melt butter in small saucepan over low heat; add nuts. Cook and stir until lightly browned. Remove from heat; stir in sugar, cocoa and salt. Stir in light cream.

2. Cook over low heat, stirring constantly, until mixture just begins to boil. Remove from heat; stir in vanilla. Serve warm.

Makes about 1 cup sauce

Cocoa in Cooking & Baking

Hot Cocoa Mix

Makes 3³/₄ cups mix (about fifteen 6-ounce servings)

2 cups nonfat dry milk powder

³/₄ cup sugar

¹/₂ cup HERSHEY'S Cocoa

¹/₂ cup powdered non-dairy creamer

Dash salt

Combine all ingredients in large bowl; stir to blend well. Store in tightly covered container.

Single Serving: Place ¹/₄ cup mix in heatproof cup or mug; add ³/₄ cup boiling water. Stir to blend. Serve hot, topped with marshmallows, if desired.

Ranch-Style Shrimp and Bacon Appetizers

RANCH-STYLE BARBECUE SAUCE (recipe follows)

30 large peeled, deveined shrimp

$^1/_2$ pound thick-cut bacon

10 wooden skewers*

To prevent wooden skewers from burning while grilling or broiling, soak in water about 10 minutes before using.

1. Prepare RANCH-STYLE BARBECUE SAUCE.

2. Wrap each shrimp with $^1/_2$ bacon strip. Thread 3 wrapped shrimp onto each wooden skewer.

3. Grill or broil shrimp skewers until bacon is cooked and shrimp is no longer translucent, but has turned pink. Baste with RANCH-STYLE BARBECUE SAUCE. Return to heat to warm sauce. Serve with additional RANCH-STYLE BARBECUE SAUCE, if desired.

Ranch-Style Barbecue Sauce

$^1/_4$ cup vegetable or olive oil

$^1/_2$ cup minced onion

2 cloves garlic, minced

2 tablespoons lemon juice

1 tablespoon ground black pepper

1 teaspoon dry mustard

1 teaspoon paprika

$^1/_2$ teaspoon salt

$^1/_2$ teaspoon hot pepper sauce

$1^1/_2$ cups ketchup

1 cup HEATH BITS 'O BRICKLE Toffee Bits

$^1/_4$ cup cider vinegar

3 tablespoons sugar

$1^1/_2$ tablespoons HERSHEY'S Cocoa

1. Heat oil in large saucepan over medium heat; add onion and garlic. Cook until tender. Stir in lemon juice, black pepper, mustard, paprika, salt and hot pepper sauce. Simmer for 5 minutes; reduce heat.

2. Stir in ketchup, toffee bits, vinegar, sugar and cocoa. Simmer 15 minutes. Refrigerate leftovers.

Makes 3 cups sauce

HERSHEY'S® Secret Ingredient Chili

1/4 cup vegetable oil

1 1/2 cups chopped onion

2 pounds lean ground beef or ground turkey

2 tablespoons HERSHEY'S Cocoa

2 tablespoons chili powder

2 teaspoons ground cayenne pepper

1 teaspoon salt

1/2 teaspoon ground allspice

1/2 teaspoon ground cinnamon

2 cans (28 ounces each) whole tomatoes, undrained

1 can (12 ounces) tomato paste

1 cup water

2 cans (about 15 ounces each) red kidney beans, drained (optional)

Additional chopped onion (optional)

Shredded Cheddar cheese (optional)

1. In 5-quart saucepan, over medium heat, heat oil; add onion. Cook, stirring frequently, 3 minutes or until tender. Add meat; cook until brown. Drain.

2. Stir in cocoa, seasonings, tomatoes with liquid, tomato paste and water; heat to boiling. Reduce heat; simmer 30 minutes.

3. Serve plain, topped with beans, sprinkled with additional chopped onion, topped with cheese or all of the above.

Cocoa in Cooking & Baking

Cocoa Spiced Beef Stir-Fry

2 **cups beef broth**

3 **tablespoons soy sauce**

2 **tablespoons cornstarch**

2 **tablespoons HERSHEY'S Cocoa**

2 **teaspoons minced garlic (about 4 cloves)**

1½ **teaspoons ground ginger**

1 **teaspoon crushed red pepper flakes**

1 **pound boneless beef top round or flank steak**

3 **tablespoons vegetable oil, divided**

1½ **cups large onion pieces**

1 **cup carrot slices**

3 **cups fresh broccoli florets and pieces**

1½ **cups sweet red pepper slices**

Hot cooked rice

Additional soy sauce

Cashew or peanut pieces (optional)

1. Stir together beef broth, soy sauce, cornstarch, cocoa, garlic, ginger and red pepper flakes; set aside. Cut beef steak into ¼-inch-wide strips.

2. Heat large skillet or wok over high heat about 1 minute or until hot. Drizzle about 1 tablespoon oil into pan; heat about 30 seconds. Add beef strips; stir-fry until well browned. Remove from heat; set aside.

3. Drizzle remaining 2 tablespoons oil into pan; add onion pieces and carrots. Stir-fry until onion is crisp, but tender. Add broccoli and red pepper strips; cook until crisp-tender.

4. Return beef to pan; add broth mixture. Cook and stir until mixture comes to a boil and thickens. Serve over hot rice with additional soy sauce and cashew pieces, if desired.

Cocoa Brunch Rings

Makes 2 rings

$^1/_2$ **cup milk**

$^1/_2$ **cup sugar**

 1 **teaspoon salt**

$^1/_2$ **cup (1 stick) butter or margarine**

 2 **packages active dry yeast**

$^1/_2$ **cup warm water**

 2 **eggs, slightly beaten**

$3^1/_2$ **to $3^3/_4$ cups all-purpose flour, divided**

$^3/_4$ **cup HERSHEY'S Cocoa**

    ORANGE FILLING (recipe follows)

1. Scald milk in small saucepan over medium heat; stir in sugar, salt and butter. Cool to lukewarm.

2. Dissolve yeast in warm water (105°F to 115°F) in large bowl; add milk mixture, eggs and 2 cups of the flour. Beat on medium speed of mixer 2 minutes until smooth. Stir together $1^1/_2$ cups of the flour and the cocoa; stir into yeast mixture.

3. Turn dough out onto well-floured board; knead in more flour until dough is smooth enough to handle. Knead about 5 minutes or until smooth and elastic. Place in greased bowl; turn dough to grease top. Cover; let rise in warm place until doubled, about 1 to $1^1/_2$ hours. Punch down dough; turn over. Cover; let rise 30 minutes longer. Prepare ORANGE FILLING; set aside.

4. Heat oven to 350°F. Grease two 4- to 6-cup ring molds. Divide dough in half. On lightly floured board, roll out each half to a 9×13-inch rectangle. Spread one-fourth of ORANGE FILLING on each rectangle to within $^1/_2$ inch of edges; reserve remaining filling for frosting. Roll up dough from long side as for jelly roll; pinch edge to seal. Cut rolls into 1-inch slices. Place slices, sealed edges down, in prepared ring molds. Tilt slices slightly, overlapping so filling shows. Cover; let rise in warm place until doubled, about 45 minutes.

5. Bake 20 to 25 minutes or until golden brown. Immediately remove from molds and place on serving plates. Frost with remaining ORANGE FILLING or, if a glaze is preferred, stir in a few drops orange juice; spoon over rings. Serve warm.

Orange Filling

- **3 cups powdered sugar**
- **6 tablespoons butter or margarine, softened**
- **3 tablespoons orange juice**
- **3 to 4 teaspoons freshly grated orange peel**

Combine powdered sugar, butter, orange juice and orange peel in medium bowl; beat on low speed until smooth.

Makes about 2 cups filling

Cocoa-Coffee Spiced Chicken with Salsa Mole

2 tablespoons ground coffee

2 tablespoons HERSHEY'S Cocoa

1 tablespoon packed light brown sugar

1½ to 2 teaspoons salt

1 teaspoon chili powder

4 boneless, skinless chicken breasts

1 tablespoon vegetable oil

SALSA MOLE (recipe follows)

Cilantro sprigs (optional)

Black beans (optional)

Rice (optional)

1. Heat oven to 425°F. Grease baking sheet.

2. Stir together coffee, cocoa, brown sugar, salt and chili powder. Rub chicken pieces with vegetable oil; pat on cocoa mixture. Place coated chicken pieces on prepared baking sheet.

3. Bake 20 to 25 minutes or until juices are clear. Meanwhile, prepare SALSA MOLE.

4. Arrange chicken and salsa on large platter. Garnish with cilantro sprigs, if desired. Serve with black beans and rice, if desired.

Salsa Mole

2 tomatoes, chopped

1 avocado, peeled and diced

1 green onion, minced

1 tablespoon snipped cilantro

1 clove garlic, pressed

¼ cup HERSHEY'S Mini Chips Semi-Sweet Chocolate

1 teaspoon lime juice

Stir together tomatoes, avocado, onion, cilantro, garlic, small chocolate chips and lime juice in medium bowl.

Berry-Berry Brownie Torte

Makes 8 to 10 servings

1/2 **cup all-purpose flour**

1/4 **teaspoon baking soda**

1/4 **teaspoon salt**

1 **cup HERSHEY'S SPECIAL DARK Chocolate Chips or HERSHEY'S Semi-Sweet Chocolate Chips**

1/2 **cup (1 stick) butter or margarine**

1 1/4 **cups sugar, divided**

2 **eggs**

1 **teaspoon vanilla extract**

1/3 **cup HERSHEY'S SPECIAL DARK Cocoa or HERSHEY'S Cocoa**

1/2 **cup whipping cream**

3/4 **cup fresh blackberries, rinsed and patted dry**

3/4 **cup fresh raspberries, rinsed and patted dry**

1. Heat oven to 350°F. Line 9-inch round baking pan with wax paper, then grease. Stir together flour, baking soda and salt. Stir in chocolate chips.

2. Melt butter in medium saucepan over low heat. Remove from heat. Stir in 1 cup sugar, eggs and vanilla. Add cocoa, blending well. Stir in flour mixture. Spread mixture in prepared pan.

3. Bake 20 to 25 minutes or until wooden pick inserted into center comes out slightly sticky. Cool in pan on wire rack 15 minutes. Invert onto wire rack; remove wax paper. Turn right side up; cool completely.

4. Beat whipping cream and remaining 1/4 cup sugar until sugar is dissolved and stiff peaks form. Spread over top of brownie. Top with berries. Refrigerate until serving time.

Chicken Satay Skewers

Makes 15 to 20 appetizers or 4 to 6 entrée servings

6 cloves garlic, chopped

4 teaspoons dried coriander

4 teaspoons light brown sugar

2 teaspoons salt

1½ teaspoons HERSHEY'S Cocoa

1 teaspoon ground black pepper

½ cup soy sauce

6 tablespoons vegetable oil

2 tablespoons lime juice

4 teaspoons fresh chopped ginger

2½ pounds boneless, skinless chicken breasts

PEANUT DIPPING SAUCE (recipe follows)

¼ cup fresh cilantro, chopped (optional)

1. Combine garlic, coriander, brown sugar, salt, cocoa and pepper in large bowl. Stir in soy sauce, oil, lime juice and ginger.

2. Cut chicken into 1½- to 2-inch cubes. Add to soy sauce mixture, stirring to coat chicken pieces. Cover; marinate in refrigerator for at least 2 hours.

3. Meanwhile, prepare PEANUT DIPPING SAUCE. Thread chicken pieces onto skewers. Grill or broil, basting with marinade. Discard leftover marinade. Garnish with chopped cilantro, if desired. Serve with PEANUT DIPPING SAUCE. Refrigerate leftovers.

Peanut Dipping Sauce

½ cup peanut oil

1 cup REESE'S Creamy Peanut Butter

¼ cup lime juice

¼ cup soy sauce

3 tablespoons honey

2 cloves garlic, minced

1 teaspoon cayenne pepper

½ teaspoon hot pepper sauce

Gradually whisk peanut oil into peanut butter in medium bowl. Blend in lime juice, soy sauce, honey, garlic, cayenne pepper and hot pepper sauce. Adjust flavors to taste for a sweet/hot flavor.

Makes about 2¼ cups dipping sauce

Fudgey Peanut Butter Chip Muffins

Makes 12 to 15 muffins

¹/₂ cup applesauce

¹/₂ cup quick-cooking rolled oats

¹/₄ cup (¹/₂ stick) butter or margarine, softened

¹/₂ cup granulated sugar

¹/₂ cup packed light brown sugar

1 egg

¹/₂ teaspoon vanilla extract

³/₄ cup all-purpose flour

¹/₄ cup HERSHEY'S SPECIAL DARK Cocoa or HERSHEY'S Cocoa

¹/₂ teaspoon baking soda

¹/₄ teaspoon ground cinnamon (optional)

1 cup REESE'S Peanut Butter Chips

Powdered sugar (optional)

1. Heat oven to 350°F. Line muffin cups (2¹/₂ inches in diameter) with paper bake cups.

2. Stir together applesauce and oats in small bowl; set aside. Beat butter, granulated sugar, brown sugar, egg and vanilla in large bowl until well blended. Add applesauce mixture; blend well. Stir together flour, cocoa, baking soda and cinnamon, if desired. Add to butter mixture, blending well. Stir in peanut butter chips. Fill muffin cups ³/₄ full with batter.

3. Bake 22 to 26 minutes or until wooden pick inserted in center comes out almost clean. Cool slightly in pan on wire rack. Sprinkle muffin tops with powdered sugar, if desired. Serve warm.

Fudgey Chocolate Chip Muffins: Omit peanut butter chips. Add 1 cup HERSHEY'S SPECIAL DARK Chocolate Chips or HERSHEY'S Semi-Sweet Chocolate Chips.

Smokey Chili with Pasta

2 cups (about 6 ounces) rotelle or rotini pasta, uncooked

1 pound ground beef

1 cup chopped onion

2 cans (about 15 ounces each) red kidney beans

2 cans (10³/₄ ounces each) condensed tomato soup

2 tablespoons HERSHEY'S Cocoa

2¹/₄ teaspoons chili powder

³/₄ teaspoon ground black pepper

¹/₂ teaspoon salt

Grated Parmesan cheese (optional)

1. Cook pasta according to package directions; drain.

2. Meanwhile, cook ground beef and onion until meat is thoroughly done and onion is tender. If necessary, drain fat.

3. Stir in undrained kidney beans, soup, cocoa, chili powder, pepper and salt. Heat to boiling; reduce heat. Stir in hot pasta; heat thoroughly. Serve with Parmesan cheese, if desired.

Rich Cocoa Crinkle Cookies

2 cups granulated sugar
³/₄ cup vegetable oil
1 cup HERSHEY'S Cocoa
4 eggs
2 teaspoons vanilla extract
2¹/₃ cups all-purpose flour
2 teaspoons baking powder
¹/₂ teaspoon salt
Powdered sugar

1. Combine granulated sugar and oil in large bowl; add cocoa, beating until well blended. Beat in eggs and vanilla. Stir together flour, baking powder and salt. Gradually add to cocoa mixture, beating well.

2. Cover; refrigerate until dough is firm enough to handle, at least 6 hours.

3. Heat oven to 350°F. Lightly grease cookie sheet or line with parchment paper. Shape dough into 1-inch balls; roll in powdered sugar to coat. Place about 2 inches apart on prepared cookie sheet.

4. Bake 10 to 12 minutes or until almost no indentation remains when touched lightly and tops are crackled. Cool slightly. Remove from cookie sheet to wire rack. Cool completely.

Tex-Mex Spice Rub

$^1/_2$ **cup HEATH BITS 'O BRICKLE Toffee Bits**

$^1/_2$ **cup HERSHEY'S Cocoa**

$^1/_2$ **cup chili powder**

$^1/_4$ **cup paprika**

1 **tablespoon ground cumin**

1 **tablespoon ground coffee beans**

2 **teaspoons salt**

2 **teaspoons dried oregano leaves**

1 **teaspoon garlic powder**

1 **teaspoon red pepper flakes**

1. Place toffee bits in food processor or blender. Cover; process until toffee bits are very fine.

2. Combine toffee and remaining ingredients in medium bowl; blend well. Place in airtight container. Store in cool dry place for up to 4 months.

Hint: Use as a rub on meats, poultry and seafood. Or toss sliced vegetables such as onions, pepper and zucchini with vinaigrette-type dressing and 1 to 2 tablespoons rub; roast 20 to 30 minutes at 450°F in a shallow baking pan until vegetables are fork tender.

Hot Chocolate Soufflé

1 **cup HERSHEY'S Cocoa**
1¼ **cups sugar, divided**
½ **cup all-purpose flour**
¼ **teaspoon salt**
2 **cups milk**
6 **egg yolks, well beaten**
2 **tablespoons butter or margarine**
1 **teaspoon vanilla extract**
8 **egg whites**
¼ **teaspoon cream of tartar**
  Sweetened whipped cream

1. Move oven rack to lowest position. Heat oven to 350°F. Lightly butter 2½-quart soufflé dish; sprinkle with sugar. For collar, cut a length of heavy-duty aluminum foil to fit around soufflé dish; fold in thirds lengthwise. Lightly butter one side of foil. Attach foil, buttered side in, around outside of dish, allowing foil to extend at least 2 inches above dish. Secure foil with tape or string.

2. Stir together cocoa, 1 cup sugar, flour and salt in large saucepan; gradually stir in milk. Cook over medium heat, stirring constantly with wire whisk, until mixture boils; remove from heat. Gradually stir small amount of chocolate mixture into beaten egg yolks; blend well. Add egg mixture to chocolate mixture in pan, blending well. Cook and stir 1 minute. Add butter and vanilla, stirring until blended. Set aside; cool 20 minutes.

3. Beat egg whites with cream of tartar in large bowl until soft peaks form; gradually add remaining ¼ cup sugar, beating until stiff peaks form. Gently fold about one-third of beaten egg white mixture into chocolate mixture. Lightly fold chocolate mixture, half at a time, into remaining beaten egg white mixture just until blended; do not overfold.

4. Gently pour mixture into prepared dish; smooth top with spatula. Gently place dish in larger baking pan; pour hot water into larger pan to depth of 1 inch.

5. Bake 1 hour and 5 to 10 minutes or until puffed and set. Remove soufflé dish from water. Carefully remove foil. Serve immediately with sweetened whipped cream.

Chocolate Mousse Cake Roll

Makes 8 to 10 servings

CHOCOLATE MOUSSE FILLING (recipe follows)

- ¹/₄ **cup powdered sugar**
- 4 **eggs, separated**
- ¹/₂ **cup plus ¹/₃ cup granulated sugar, divided**
- 1 **teaspoon vanilla extract**
- ¹/₂ **cup all-purpose flour**
- ¹/₃ **cup HERSHEY'S Cocoa**
- ¹/₂ **teaspoon baking powder**
- ¹/₄ **teaspoon baking soda**
- ¹/₈ **teaspoon salt**
- ¹/₃ **cup water**

  Additional powdered sugar

  HERSHEY'S Syrup

1. Prepare CHOCOLATE MOUSSE FILLING. Chill 6 to 8 hours or overnight.

2. Prepare cake.* Heat oven to 375°F. Line 15¹/₂×10¹/₂×1-inch jelly-roll pan with foil; generously grease foil. Sprinkle linen or thin cotton towel with ¹/₄ cup powdered sugar.

3. Beat egg whites in large bowl until soft peaks form; gradually add ¹/₂ cup granulated sugar, beating until stiff peaks form. Beat egg yolks and vanilla in medium bowl on medium speed of mixer 3 minutes.

Gradually add remaining ¹/₃ cup granulated sugar; continue beating 2 additional minutes.

4. Stir together flour, cocoa, baking powder, baking soda and salt; add to egg yolk mixture alternately with water, beating on low speed just until batter is smooth. Gradually fold chocolate mixture into beaten egg whites until well blended. Spread batter evenly in prepared pan.

5. Bake 12 to 15 minutes or until top springs back when touched lightly in center. Immediately loosen cake from edges of pan; invert onto prepared towel. Carefully peel off foil. Immediately roll cake and towel together starting from narrow end; place on wire rack to cool completely.

6. Carefully unroll cake; remove towel. Gently stir FILLING until of spreading consistency. Spread cake with CHOCOLATE MOUSSE FILLING; reroll cake. Refrigerate several hours. Sift powdered sugar over top just before serving. Serve drizzled with syrup and garnished as desired. Cover; refrigerate leftover cake roll.

Cake may be prepared up to 2 days in advance. Keep cake rolled tightly and covered well so that it doesn't get dry.

Chocolate Mousse Filling

- ¹/₄ **cup sugar**
- 1 **teaspoon unflavored gelatin**
- ¹/₂ **cup milk**
- 1 **cup HERSHEY'S SPECIAL DARK Chocolate Chips or HERSHEY'S Semi-Sweet Chocolate Chips**
- 2 **teaspoons vanilla extract**
- 1 **cup (¹/₂ pint) cold whipping cream**

1. Stir together sugar and gelatin in small saucepan; stir in milk. Let stand 2 minutes to soften gelatin. Cook over medium heat, stirring constantly, until mixture just begins to boil.

2. Remove from heat. Immediately add chocolate chips; stir until melted. Stir in vanilla; cool to room temperature.

3. Beat whipping cream in small bowl until stiff. Gradually add chocolate mixture, folding gently just until blended. Cover; refrigerate until ready to use.

Makes about 3 cups filling

Spicy Cocoa Glazed Pecans

Makes 1½ cups coated pecans

¼ **cup plus 2 tablespoons sugar, divided**

1 **cup warm water**

1½ **cups pecan halves or pieces**

1 **tablespoon HERSHEY'S Cocoa**

3 **to 4 teaspoons chili powder**

⅛ **to ¼ teaspoon cayenne pepper**

1. Heat oven to 350°F. Lightly spray shallow baking pan with vegetable cooking spray.

2. Stir together ¼ cup sugar and warm water, stirring until sugar dissolves. Add pecans; let soak 10 minutes. Drain water and discard.

3. Stir together remaining 2 tablespoons sugar, cocoa, chili powder and cayenne pepper in medium bowl. Add pecans; toss until all cocoa mixture coats pecans. Spread coated pecans on prepared pan.

4. Bake 10 to 15 minutes or until pecans start to glisten and appear dry. Stir occasionally while baking. Cool completely. Store in cool, dry place. Serve as a snack with beverages or sprinkle in salads.

Chocolate Quickie Stickies

- $^1/_2$ **cup (1 stick) butter or margarine, divided**
- $^3/_4$ **cup packed light brown sugar**
- 4 **tablespoons HERSHEY'S Cocoa, divided**
- 5 **teaspoons water**
- 1 **teaspoon vanilla extract**
- $^1/_2$ **cup coarsely chopped nuts (optional)**
- 2 **cans (8 ounces each) refrigerated quick crescent dinner rolls**
- 2 **tablespoons granulated sugar**

1. Heat oven to 350°F.

2. Melt 6 tablespoons butter in small saucepan over low heat; add brown sugar, 3 tablespoons cocoa and water. Cook over medium heat, stirring constantly, just until mixture comes to boil. Remove from heat; stir in vanilla. Spoon about 1 teaspoon chocolate mixture into each of 48 small muffin cups ($1^3/_4$ inches in diameter). Sprinkle $^1/_2$ teaspoon nuts, if desired, into each cup; set aside.

3. Unroll dough; separate into 8 rectangles; firmly press perforations to seal. Melt remaining 2 tablespoons butter; brush over rectangles. Stir together granulated sugar and remaining 1 tablespoon cocoa; sprinkle over rectangles. Starting at longer side, roll up each rectangle; pinch seams to seal. Cut each roll into 6 equal pieces. Press gently into prepared pans, cut-side down.

4. Bake 11 to 13 minutes or until light brown. Remove from oven; let cool 30 seconds. Invert onto cookie sheet. Let stand 1 minute; remove pans. Serve warm or cool completely.

Note: Rolls can be baked in two 8-inch round baking pans. Heat oven to 350°F. Cook chocolate mixture as directed; spread half of mixture in each pan. Prepare rolls as directed; place 24 pieces, cut-side down, in each pan. Bake 20 to 22 minutes. Cool and remove from pans as directed above.

Ice Cream Sandwiches

$^1/_2$ **cup shortening**

1 **cup sugar**

1 **egg**

1 **teaspoon vanilla extract**

1$^2/_3$ **cups all-purpose flour**

$^1/_3$ **cup HERSHEY'S Cocoa**

$^1/_2$ **teaspoon baking soda**

$^1/_2$ **teaspoon salt**

$^1/_4$ **cup milk**

   Desired flavor ice cream, slightly softened

   Assorted chopped HERSHEY'S, REESE'S or HEATH baking pieces, crushed peppermints or other small candies (optional)

1. Beat shortening, sugar, egg and vanilla in large bowl until well blended. Stir together flour, cocoa, baking soda and salt; add alternately with milk to sugar mixture, beating until well blended. Cover; refrigerate about 1 hour.

2. Heat oven to 375°F. Drop batter by heaping tablespoons onto ungreased cookie sheet. With palm of hand or bottom of glass, flatten each cookie into 2$^3/_4$-inch circle, about $^1/_4$ inch thick. Bake 8 to 10 minutes or until almost set. Cool 1 minute; remove from cookie sheet to wire rack. Cool completely.

3. Place scoop of ice cream on flat side of 1 cookie; spread evenly with spatula. Top with another cookie, pressing together lightly; repeat with remaining cookies. Roll ice cream edges in chopped baking pieces or candies, if desired. Wrap individually in foil; freeze until firm.

Cocoa in Cooking & Baking

Cocoa Black Forest Crêpes

Makes about 18 crepes

3 **eggs**

³/₄ **cup water**

¹/₂ **cup light cream or half-and-half**

³/₄ **cup plus 2 tablespoons all-purpose flour**

3 **tablespoons HERSHEY'S Cocoa**

2 **tablespoons sugar**

¹/₈ **teaspoon salt**

3 **tablespoons butter or margarine, melted and cooled**

Cherry pie filling

CHOCOLATE SAUCE (recipe follows)

Sweetened whipped cream (optional)

1. Combine eggs, water and light cream in blender or food processor; blend 10 seconds. Add flour, cocoa, sugar, salt and butter; blend until smooth. Let stand at room temperature 30 minutes.

2. Spray 6-inch crêpe pan lightly with vegetable cooking spray; heat over medium heat. For each crêpe, pour 2 to 3 tablespoons batter into pan; lift and tilt pan to spread batter. Return to heat; cook until surface begins to dry. Loosen crêpe around edges; turn and lightly cook other side. Stack crêpes, placing wax paper between crêpes. Keep covered. (Refrigerate for later use, if desired.)

3. Just before serving, place 2 tablespoons pie filling onto each crêpe; roll up. Place crêpes on dessert plate. Prepare CHOCOLATE SAUCE; spoon over crêpes. Garnish with sweetened whipped cream, if desired.

Chocolate Sauce: Stir together ³/₄ cup sugar and ¹/₃ cup HERSHEY'S Cocoa in small saucepan; add in ¹/₂ cup plus 2 tablespoons (5-ounce can) evaporated milk, ¹/₄ cup (¹/₂ stick) butter or margarine and ¹/₈ teaspoon salt. Cook over medium heat, stirring constantly, until mixture comes to a boil. Remove from heat; stir in 1 teaspoon kirsch (cherry brandy), if desired. Serve warm. Cover; refrigerate leftover sauce. Makes about 1¹/₂ cups sauce.

Chocolate Quicky Sticky Bread

Makes 12 servings

2 loaves (16 ounces each) frozen bread dough

³/₄ cup granulated sugar

1 tablespoon HERSHEY'S Cocoa

1 teaspoon ground cinnamon

¹/₂ cup (1 stick) butter or margarine, melted and divided

¹/₂ cup packed light brown sugar

¹/₄ cup water

About 1 cup HERSHEY'S MINI KISSESBRAND Milk Chocolates

1. Thaw loaves as directed on package; let rise until doubled.

2. Stir together granulated sugar, cocoa and cinnamon. Stir together ¹/₄ cup butter, brown sugar and water in small microwave-safe bowl. Microwave at MEDIUM (50%) 30 to 60 seconds or until smooth when stirred. Pour mixture into 12-cup fluted tube pan.

3. Heat oven to 350°F. Pinch off pieces of bread dough; form into balls (1¹/₂ inches in diameter) placing 3 chocolate pieces inside each ball. Dip each ball in remaining ¹/₄ cup butter; roll in cocoa-sugar mixture. Place balls in prepared pan.

4. Bake 45 to 50 minutes or until golden brown. Cool 20 minutes in pan; invert onto serving plate. Cool until lukewarm.

Cocoa Marble Gingerbread

1/2 cup shortening

1 cup sugar

1 cup light molasses

2 eggs

1 teaspoon baking soda

1 cup boiling water

2 cups all-purpose flour

1 teaspoon salt

1/4 cup HERSHEY'S Cocoa

1/2 teaspoon ground cinnamon

1/2 teaspoon ground ginger

1/4 teaspoon ground cloves

1/4 teaspoon ground nutmeg

Sweetened whipped cream (optional)

1. Heat oven to 350°F. Grease and flour 13×9×2-inch baking pan.

2. Beat shortening, sugar and molasses in large bowl until blended. Add eggs; beat well. Stir baking soda into water to dissolve; add to shortening mixture alternately with flour and salt. Remove 2 cups batter to medium bowl; add cocoa, blending well. Add spices to remaining batter in large bowl. Alternately spoon batters into prepared pan; gently swirl through batter with narrow spatula or knife for marbled effect.

3. Bake 40 to 45 minutes or until wooden pick inserted in center comes out clean. Cut into squares. Serve warm or at room temperature with sweetened whipped cream, if desired.

Cocoa Flan

1 **cup sugar**

1 **can (5 ounces) evaporated whole milk***

Water

¹/₄ **cup HERSHEY'S Cocoa**

1 **can (14 ounces) sweetened condensed milk**

4 **eggs**

2 **teaspoons vanilla extract**

¹/₄ **teaspoon salt**

1¹/₄ cups whole milk may be substituted for the reconstituted evaporated milk.

1. Heat oven to 325°F. Heat sugar in heavy medium skillet or saucepan over medium-low heat, stirring occasionally, until melted and golden brown. Pour into bottom of 1¹/₂-quart baking dish.

2. Pour evaporated milk into 2-cup glass measuring cup; add water to make 1¹/₄ cups. Place cocoa in medium bowl; add enough of the reconstituted milk to form a paste and then gradually blend in the remaining milk.

3. Place chocolate milk mixture, sweetened condensed milk, eggs, vanilla and salt in blender container. Cover; blend until smooth and well blended. Gradually pour over sugar mixture in baking dish. Cover top of baking dish with foil to keep it from browning.

4. Set dish in a larger baking pan. Fill the larger pan with water until it reaches halfway up sides of dish. Bake 1¹/₂ to 2 hours or until knife comes out almost clean when inserted halfway into center of custard. (Do not pierce bottom.) Remove from water to wire rack. Cool 2 hours. Cover; refrigerate overnight or until thoroughly chilled (about 8 hours).

5. To serve, run a knife or rubber scraper along the outside of the flan. Place serving plate over baking dish; invert onto serving plate. Let stand several minutes for the flan to release and the topping to drip down; remove baking dish. Garnish as desired.

Rich Cocoa Fudge

Makes about 3 dozen pieces or 1³/₄ pounds candy

3 cups sugar

²/₃ cup HERSHEY'S Cocoa or HERSHEY'S SPECIAL DARK Cocoa

¹/₈ teaspoon salt

1¹/₂ cups milk

¹/₄ cup (¹/₂ stick) butter

1 teaspoon vanilla extract

1. Line 8- or 9-inch square pan with foil, extending foil over edges of pan. Butter foil.

2. Stir together sugar, cocoa and salt in heavy 4-quart saucepan; stir in milk. Cook over medium heat, stirring constantly, until mixture comes to full rolling boil. Boil, without stirring, until mixture reaches 234°F on candy thermometer or until small amount of mixture dropped into very cold water forms a soft ball which flattens when removed from water. (Bulb of candy thermometer should not rest on bottom of saucepan.) Remove from heat.

3. Add butter and vanilla. DO NOT STIR. Cool at room temperature to 110°F (lukewarm). Beat with wooden spoon until fudge thickens and just begins to lose some of its gloss. Quickly spread in prepared pan; cool completely. Cut into squares. Store in tightly covered container at room temperature.

Nutty Rich Cocoa Fudge:
Beat cooked fudge as directed. Immediately stir in 1 cup chopped almonds, pecans or walnuts and quickly spread in prepared pan.

Marshmallow Nut Cocoa Fudge:
Increase cocoa to ³/₄ cup. Cook fudge as directed. Add 1 cup marshmallow creme with butter and vanilla. DO NOT STIR. Cool to 110°F (lukewarm). Beat 8 minutes; stir in 1 cup chopped nuts. Pour into prepared pan. (Fudge does not set until poured into pan.)

Notes: For best results, do not double this recipe. This is one of our most requested recipes, but also one of our most difficult. The directions must be followed exactly. Beat too little and the fudge is too soft. Beat too long and it becomes hard and sugary.

Chocolate Oatmeal Walnut Muffins

Makes about 14 muffins

1 cup quick-cooking rolled oats

1 cup buttermilk or sour milk*

$^2/_3$ cup light packed brown sugar

$^1/_3$ cup vegetable oil

1 egg

1 teaspoon vanilla extract

$^3/_4$ cup all-purpose flour

$^1/_4$ cup HERSHEY'S Cocoa

1 teaspoon baking powder

1 teaspoon salt

$^1/_2$ teaspoon baking soda

1 cup coarsely chopped walnuts

Powdered sugar (optional)

*To sour milk: Use 1 tablespoon white vinegar plus milk to equal 1 cup.

1. Heat oven to 400°F. Grease or line muffin cups ($2^1/_2$ inches in diameter) with paper bake cups.

2. Stir together oats and buttermilk in small bowl; let stand 20 minutes.

3. Stir together brown sugar, oil, egg and vanilla in large bowl. Add oats mixture, stirring well. Stir together flour, cocoa, baking powder, salt and baking soda. Add to oats mixture, blending until moistened. Stir in nuts. Fill muffin cups $^2/_3$ full with batter.

4. Bake 16 to 18 minutes or until wooden pick inserted in center comes out clean. Remove from pan to wire rack. Sprinkle muffin tops with powdered sugar, if desired. Serve warm or cool.

Orange Cocoa Cake

¹/₂ cup **HERSHEY'S Cocoa**

¹/₂ cup **boiling water**

¹/₄ cup **(¹/₂ stick) butter or margarine, softened**

¹/₄ cup **shortening**

2 cups **sugar**

¹/₈ teaspoon **salt**

1 teaspoon **vanilla extract**

2 **eggs**

1¹/₂ teaspoons **baking soda**

1 cup **buttermilk or sour milk***

1³/₄ cups **all-purpose flour**

3 tablespoons **buttermilk or sour milk***

¹/₈ teaspoon **baking soda**

³/₄ teaspoon **freshly grated orange peel**

¹/₄ teaspoon **orange extract**

ORANGE BUTTERCREAM FROSTING (recipe follows)

*To sour milk: Use 1 tablespoon vinegar plus milk to equal 1 cup; use ¹/₂ teaspoon vinegar plus milk to equal 3 tablespoons.

1. Heat oven to 350°F. Grease three 8- or 9-inch layer pans and line bottoms with wax paper; set aside.

2. Stir together cocoa and boiling water in small bowl until smooth; set aside. Beat butter, shortening, sugar, salt and vanilla in large bowl until well blended. Add eggs; beat well. Stir 1¹/₂ teaspoons baking soda into 1 cup buttermilk; add alternately with flour to butter mixture.

3. Measure 1²/₃ cups batter into small bowl. Stir in 3 tablespoons buttermilk, ¹/₈ teaspoon baking soda, the orange peel and orange extract; pour into one prepared pan. Stir cocoa mixture into remaining batter; divide evenly between remaining two prepared pans.

4. Bake 25 to 30 minutes or until wooden pick inserted in center comes out clean. Cool 10 minutes; remove from pans. Carefully peel off wax paper. Cool completely.

5. Place one chocolate layer on serving plate; spread with some of the ORANGE BUTTERCREAM FROSTING. Top with orange layer and spread with frosting. Top with remaining chocolate layer and frost entire cake.

Orange Buttercream Frosting

- **²/₃ cup butter or margarine, softened**
- **6 cups powdered sugar**
- **2 teaspoons freshly grated orange peel**
- **1¹/₂ teaspoons vanilla extract**
- **4 to 6 tablespoons milk**

Beat butter, 1 cup powdered sugar, the orange peel and vanilla in large bowl. Add remaining powdered sugar alternately with milk, beating to spreading consistency. If necessary, add additional milk, ¹/₂ teaspoon at a time, to get desired spreading consistency.

Makes about 3 cups frosting

Holiday Treats

Drinking Chocolate

2 sections (¹/₂ ounce each) HERSHEY'S Unsweetened Chocolate Baking Bar

2 tablespoons hot water

¹/₄ cup sugar

Dash of salt

¹/₄ cup milk, warmed

¹/₄ teaspoon vanilla extract

Place chocolate and water in top of small double boiler. Melt over simmering water, stirring until smooth. Stir in sugar and salt, blending thoroughly. Gradually blend in warm milk. Heat, stirring occasionally, until hot. Stir in vanilla. Pour into demitasse cups. Garnish as desired. Serve immediately.

Holiday Treats

Toffee Scones Mix

3¼ cups all-purpose flour

½ cup sugar

1 tablespoon plus 1 teaspoon baking powder

¼ teaspoon salt

1⅓ cups (8-ounce package) HEATH BITS 'O BRICKLE Toffee Bits

½ cup toasted chopped walnuts*

BAKING INSTRUCTIONS (recipe follows)

*To toast walnuts: Heat oven to 350°F. Spread walnuts in thin layer in shallow baking pan. Bake 8 to 10 minutes, stirring occasionally. Cool.

1. Stir together flour, sugar, baking powder, salt, toffee bits and walnuts. Place in 1-quart heavy-duty resealable plastic food storage bag. Press out air; seal. (Ingredients may also be layered in tightly sealed glass container.)

2. Place toffee baking mix bag in decorative gift bag or container. Attach BAKING INSTRUCTIONS.

Baking Instructions:

1. Heat oven to 375°F. Line 2 baking sheets with parchment paper or lightly grease.

2. Empty contents of toffee baking mix into large bowl. Stir 2 cups (1 pint) whipping cream into mixture, stirring just until ingredients are moistened.

3. Turn mixture out onto lightly floured surface. Knead gently until soft dough forms (about 2 minutes). Divide dough into three equal balls. One ball at a time, flatten into 7-inch circle; cut into 8 triangles. Transfer triangles to prepared baking sheets, spacing 2 inches apart. Brush with melted butter and sprinkle with sugar.

4. Bake 15 to 20 minutes or until lightly browned. Serve warm or cool.

Pears with Chocolate-Orange Sauce

Makes 6 servings

6 fresh pears
1¹/₂ cups apple juice
1 teaspoon vanilla extract
CHOCOLATE-ORANGE SAUCE (recipe follows)

1. Slice piece off bottom of pears to make a flat base. Peel pears and core from bottom but leave stems intact.

2. Combine juice with vanilla in large saucepan; add pears, base side down. Heat to boiling; reduce heat. Cover; simmer, spooning juice over pears occasionally, 20 to 25 minutes or until pears are tender.

3. Meanwhile, prepare CHOCOLATE-ORANGE SAUCE. To serve, place pear, base side down, in serving dish; spoon about 1 tablespoon warm sauce over top.

Chocolate-Orange Sauce

³/₄ cup HERSHEY'S SPECIAL DARK Chocolate Chips or HERSHEY'S Semi-Sweet Chocolate Chips

1 tablespoon shortening (do not use butter, margarine, spread or oil)

¹/₄ teaspoon orange extract

Place all ingredients in medium microwave-safe bowl. Microwave at MEDIUM (50%) 30 seconds; stir. If necessary, microwave at MEDIUM an additional 10 seconds at a time, stirring after each heating, until chocolate is melted and mixture is smooth when stirred. Serve warm sauce over hot poached pears.

Makes ¹/₂ cup sauce

Holiday Treats

European Mocha Fudge Cake

1¼ cups (2½ sticks) butter or margarine

¾ cup HERSHEY'S SPECIAL DARK Cocoa

4 eggs

¼ teaspoon salt

1 teaspoon vanilla extract

2 cups sugar

1 cup all-purpose flour

1 cup finely chopped pecans

CREAMY COFFEE FILLING (recipe follows)

Chocolate curls (optional)

1. Heat oven to 350°F. Butter bottom and sides of two 9-inch round baking pans. Line bottoms with wax paper; butter paper.

2. Melt butter in small saucepan; remove from heat. Add cocoa, stirring until blended; cool slightly. Beat eggs in large bowl until foamy; add salt and vanilla. Gradually add sugar, beating well. Add cooled chocolate mixture; blend thoroughly. Fold in flour. Stir in pecans. Pour mixture into prepared pans.

3. Bake 20 to 25 minutes or until wooden pick inserted in center comes out clean. Do not overbake. Cool 5 minutes; remove from pans to wire racks. Carefully peel off paper. Cool completely. Spread CREAMY COFFEE FILLING between layers, over top and sides of cake. Garnish with chocolate curls, if desired. Refrigerate 1 hour or longer before serving. Cover leftover cake; store in refrigerator.

Make Ahead Directions: Cooled cake may be wrapped and frozen up to 4 weeks; thaw, wrapped, before filling and frosting.

Creamy Coffee Filling

1½ cups cold whipping cream

⅓ cup packed light brown sugar

2 teaspoons powdered instant coffee

Combine all ingredients; stir until instant coffee is almost dissolved. Beat until stiff.

Makes about 3 cups filling

Macadamia Nut Fudge

1½ cups sugar

1 jar (7 ounces) marshmallow creme

1 can (5 ounces) evaporated milk (about ⅔ cup)

¼ cup (½ stick) butter or margarine

2 cups (12-ounce package) HERSHEY'S SPECIAL DARK Chocolate Chips

1 cup MAUNA LOA Macadamia Nut Baking Pieces

½ teaspoon vanilla extract

1. Line 8- or 9-inch square pan with foil, extending foil over edges of pan.

2. Combine sugar, marshmallow creme, evaporated milk and butter in heavy medium saucepan. Cook over medium heat, stirring constantly, to a full boil. Boil, stirring constantly, 5 minutes.

3. Remove from heat; add chocolate chips. Stir just until chips are melted. Stir in nuts and vanilla; pour into prepared pan.

4. Refrigerate 1 hour or until firm. Lift fudge out of pan using foil; place on cutting board. Cut into squares. Store tightly covered in a cool, dry place.

Note: For best results, do not double this recipe.

HERSHEY'S® Chocolate Peppermint Roll

CHOCOLATE SPONGE ROLL

- $^1/_4$ **cup powdered sugar**
- **4 eggs, separated**
- $^1/_2$ **cup plus $^1/_3$ cup granulated sugar, divided**
- **1 teaspoon vanilla extract**
- $^1/_2$ **cup all-purpose flour**
- $^1/_3$ **cup HERSHEY'S Cocoa**
- $^1/_2$ **teaspoon baking powder**
- $^1/_4$ **teaspoon baking soda**
- $^1/_8$ **teaspoon salt**
- $^1/_3$ **cup water**

PEPPERMINT FILLING

- **1 cup ($^1/_2$ pint) whipping cream, cold**
- $^1/_4$ **cup powdered sugar**
- $^1/_4$ **cup finely crushed hard peppermint candy or $^1/_2$ teaspoon mint extract**
- **Few drops red food color (optional)**

CHOCOLATE GLAZE

- **2 tablespoons butter or margarine**
- **2 tablespoons HERSHEY'S Cocoa**
- **2 tablespoons water**
- **1 cup powdered sugar**
- $^1/_2$ **teaspoon vanilla extract**

1. For CHOCOLATE SPONGE ROLL, heat oven to 375°F. Line 15$^1/_2$×10$^1/_2$×1-inch jelly-roll pan with foil; generously grease foil. Sprinkle linen or thin cotton towel with $^1/_4$ cup powdered sugar.

2. Beat egg whites with electric mixer on high speed in large bowl until soft peaks form; gradually add $^1/_2$ cup granulated sugar, beating until stiff peaks form. Set aside.

3. Beat egg yolks and vanilla with electric mixer on medium speed in medium bowl 3 minutes. Gradually add remaining $^1/_3$ cup granulated sugar; continue beating 2 minutes. Stir together flour, cocoa, baking powder, baking soda and salt. With mixer on low speed, add flour mixture to egg yolk mixture alternately with water, beating just until batter is smooth. Using rubber spatula, gradually fold beaten egg whites into chocolate mixture until well blended. Spread batter evenly in prepared pan.

4. Bake 12 to 15 minutes or until top springs back when touched lightly. Immediately loosen cake from edges of pan; invert onto prepared towel. Carefully peel off foil. Immediately roll cake in towel, starting from narrow end; place on wire rack to cool completely.

5. For PEPPERMINT FILLING, beat whipping cream with electric mixer on medium speed in medium bowl until slightly thickened. Add ¼ cup powdered sugar and peppermint candy or mint extract and food color, if desired; beat cream until stiff peaks form.

6. For CHOCOLATE GLAZE, melt butter in small saucepan over very low heat; add cocoa and water, stirring until smooth and slightly thickened. Remove from heat and cool slightly. (Cool completely for thicker frosting.) Gradually beat in 1 cup powdered sugar and vanilla.

7. Carefully unroll cake; remove towel. Spread cake with PEPPERMINT FILLING; reroll cake. Glaze with CHOCOLATE GLAZE. Refrigerate until just before serving. Cover; refrigerate leftover dessert.

Variation: Substitute COFFEE FILLING for PEPPERMINT FILLING. Combine 1½ cups cold milk and 2 teaspoons powdered instant coffee in medium bowl; let stand 5 minutes. Add 1 package (4-serving size) instant vanilla pudding. Beat with electric mixer on lowest speed about 2 minutes or until well blended. Use as directed above to fill CHOCOLATE SPONGE ROLL.

Holiday Treats

REESE'S® Peanut Butter Bark

2 packages (4 ounces each) HERSHEY'S Semi-Sweet Chocolate Baking Bars, broken into pieces

1²/₃ cups (10-ounce package) REESE'S Peanut Butter Chips

1 tablespoon shortening (do not use butter, margarine, spread or oil)

¹/₂ cup roasted peanuts or toasted almonds,* coarsely chopped

To toast almonds: Heat oven to 350°F. Spread almonds in thin layer in shallow baking pan. Bake 8 to 10 minutes, stirring occasionally, until light golden brown; cool.

1. Cover tray with wax paper.

2. Place chocolate in medium microwave-safe bowl. Microwave at MEDIUM (50%) 1 minute; stir. If necessary, microwave at MEDIUM an additional 30 seconds at a time, stirring after each heating, until chocolate is melted and smooth when stirred.

3. Immediately place peanut butter chips and shortening in second microwave-safe bowl. Microwave at MEDIUM 1 minute; stir. If necessary, microwave at MEDIUM an additional 30 seconds at a time, stirring after each heating, until chips are melted and mixture is smooth when stirred; stir in peanuts.

4. Alternately spoon above mixtures onto prepared tray; swirl with knife for marbled effect. Gently tap tray on countertop to even thickness of mixture. Cover; refrigerate until firm. Break into pieces.

Buche de Noel Cookies

- ²/₃ **cup butter or margarine, softened**
- 1 **cup granulated sugar**
- 2 **eggs**
- 2 **teaspoons vanilla extract**
- 2¹/₂ **cups all-purpose flour**
- ¹/₂ **cup HERSHEY'S Cocoa**
- ¹/₂ **teaspoon baking soda**
- ¹/₄ **teaspoon salt**
- **MOCHA FROSTING (recipe follows)**
- **Powdered sugar (optional)**

1. Beat butter and granulated sugar with electric mixer on medium speed in large bowl until well blended. Add eggs and vanilla; beat until fluffy. Stir together flour, cocoa, baking soda and salt; gradually add to butter mixture, beating until well blended. Cover; refrigerate dough 1 to 2 hours.

2. Heat oven to 350°F. Shape heaping teaspoons of dough into logs about 2¹/₂ inches long and ³/₄ inches in diameter; place on ungreased cookie sheet. Bake 7 to 9 minutes or until set. Cool slightly. Remove to wire rack and cool completely.

3. Frost cookies with MOCHA FROSTING. Using tines of fork, draw lines through frosting to imitate tree bark. Lightly dust with powdered sugar, if desired.

Mocha Frosting

- 6 **tablespoons butter or margarine, softened**
- 2²/₃ **cups powdered sugar**
- ¹/₃ **cup HERSHEY'S Cocoa**
- 3 **to 4 tablespoons milk**
- 2 **teaspoons powdered instant espresso dissolved in 1 teaspoon hot water**
- 1 **teaspoon vanilla extract**

Beat butter with electric mixer on medium speed in medium bowl until creamy. Add powdered sugar and cocoa alternately with milk, dissolved espresso and vanilla, beating to spreadable consistency.

Makes about 1²/₃ cups frosting

Easy Chocolate Cream Filled Torte

1 **frozen pound cake (10³/₄ ounces), thawed**

¹/₂ **cup powdered sugar**

¹/₄ **cup HERSHEY'S Cocoa**

1 **cup (¹/₂ pint) cold whipping cream**

1 **teaspoon vanilla extract**

CHOCOLATE GLAZE (recipe follows)

Sliced almonds (optional)

1. Cut cake horizontally to make 4 layers. Stir together sugar and cocoa in medium bowl. Add whipping cream and vanilla; beat until stiff.

2. Place bottom cake layer on serving platter. Spread ¹/₃ of the whipped cream mixture on cake layer. Place next cake layer on top of mixture; continue layering whipped cream mixture and cake until all have been used.

3. Prepare CHOCOLATE GLAZE; spoon over top of cake, allowing to drizzle down sides. Garnish with almonds, if desired. Refrigerate until ready to serve. Cover; refrigerate leftover torte.

Chocolate Glaze

2 **tablespoons butter or margarine**

2 **tablespoons HERSHEY'S Cocoa**

2 **tablespoons water**

1 **cup powdered sugar**

¹/₄ **to ¹/₂ teaspoon almond extract**

1. Melt butter in small saucepan over low heat. Add cocoa and water. Cook, stirring constantly, until smooth and slightly thickened. Do not boil.

2. Remove from heat. Gradually add powdered sugar and almond extract, beating with whisk until smooth.

Makes about ¹/₂ cup glaze

KISSES® Christmas Candies

About 14 HERSHEY'S KISSESBRAND **Milk Chocolates**

³/₄ **cup ground almonds**

¹/₃ **cup powdered sugar**

1 **tablespoon light corn syrup**

¹/₂ **teaspoon almond extract**

Few drops green food color

Few drops red food color

Granulated sugar

1. Remove wrappers from chocolates. Stir together ground almonds and powdered sugar in medium bowl until well blended. Stir together corn syrup and almond extract; stir or mix with hands until completely blended. Divide mixture in half, placing each half in separate bowls.

2. Add green food color to one part; with hands, mix until color is well blended and mixture clings together. Add red food color to other half; mix as directed.

3. Shape at least 1 teaspoon colored almond mixture around each chocolate. Roll in granulated sugar. Store in airtight container in cool, dry place.

Festive Fudge

3 cups (1$\frac{1}{2}$ packages, 11.5 ounces each) HERSHEY'S Milk Chocolate Chips

1 can (14 ounces) sweetened condensed milk (not evaporated milk)

Dash salt

$\frac{1}{2}$ to 1 cup chopped nuts (optional)

1$\frac{1}{2}$ teaspoons vanilla extract

1. Line 8- or 9-inch square pan with wax paper.

2. Melt chocolate chips with sweetened condensed milk and salt in heavy saucepan over low heat. Remove from heat; stir in nuts, if desired, and vanilla. Spread evenly in prepared pan.

3. Refrigerate 2 hours or until firm. Turn fudge onto cutting board; peel off paper and cut into squares. Store covered in refrigerator.

Chocolate Peanut Butter Chip Glazed Fudge: Proceed as above; stir in $\frac{2}{3}$ cup REESE'S Peanut Butter Chips in place of nuts. Melt 1 cup REESE'S Peanut Butter Chips with $\frac{1}{2}$ cup whipping cream; stir until thick and smooth. Spread over fudge.

Semi-Sweet Festive Fudge: Proceed as above using 3 cups (1$\frac{1}{2}$ packages, 12 ounces each) HERSHEY'S SPECIAL DARK Chocolate Chips or HERSHEY'S Semi-Sweet Chocolate Chips.

Chocolate Peanut Butter Chip Glazed Fudge

Mocha Molten Chocolate Cake

FROZEN CHOCOLATE CENTER (recipe follows)

2 **teaspoons powdered instant coffee**

1/4 **cup water**

1 **cup all-purpose flour**

1/2 **cup plus 1 tablespoon HERSHEY'S Cocoa**

1/8 **teaspoon salt**

3/4 **cup (1½ sticks) plus 2 tablespoons butter, softened**

1¼ **cups granulated sugar, divided**

2 **teaspoons vanilla extract**

3 **eggs**

MOCHA CREAM (recipe follows)

Powdered sugar

1. Prepare FROZEN CHOCOLATE CENTER.

2. Heat oven to 425°F. Butter sides and bottom of four (6-ounce) ramekins. Place on baking sheet.

3. Dissolve instant coffee in water; set aside. Stir together flour, cocoa and salt; set aside.

4. Beat butter in large bowl with electric mixer until light and fluffy. Set aside 1 tablespoon granulated sugar; gradually beat in remaining granulated sugar, vanilla and dissolved coffee, beating thoroughly.

5. Separate egg yolks from the egg whites. One at a time, add egg yolks to butter mixture, beating well after each addition.

6. In separate bowl, beat egg whites at low speed until frothy. Gradually increasing to high speed, beat the whites until soft peaks start to form. Add remaining 1 tablespoon granulated sugar, 1 teaspoon at a time, beating until stiff, shiny peaks form.

7. Fold 1/3 of the cocoa mixture and 1/3 of the egg whites into the butter mixture. One-half at a time, gently fold remaining cocoa mixture and egg whites into mixture.

8. Spoon about 2/3 cup batter into each ramekin. Place heaping teaspoon FROZEN CHOCOLATE CENTER mixture on center of each batter-filled ramekin. Spoon about 1/4 cup of remaining batter over FROZEN CHOCOLATE CENTER making sure to cover completely.

9. Bake 15 to 20 minutes or until tops have started to crack.

10. While cakes are baking, reheat remaining FROZEN CHOCOLATE CENTER and make MOCHA CREAM.

11. To serve, carefully invert cake onto large dinner plate. Spoon MOCHA CREAM around base of cake; dust with powdered sugar. Garnish as desired. Serve immediately with the warmed chocolate sauce.

Frozen Chocolate Center

- 1 **cup HERSHEY'S SPECIAL DARK Chocolate Chips**
- 1 **teaspoon powdered instant coffee**
- ³/₄ **cup heavy cream**
- 2 **tablespoons light corn syrup**
- 1 **teaspoon vanilla extract**

Place chocolate chips and instant coffee in medium mixing bowl. Stir together cream and corn syrup in medium saucepan. Cook over medium heat, stirring constantly with wooden spoon until mixture comes to a boil. Pour hot cream over chocolate, let stand 30 seconds; stir until chocolate is melted and mixture is smooth. Stir in vanilla. Pour chocolate mixture into shallow bowl or dish. Cool slightly. Freeze at least 3 to 4 hours (mixture will not freeze completely).

Mocha Cream

- 1 **cup (¹/₂ pint) whipping cream**
- 3 **tablespoons powdered sugar**
- 1 **tablespoon HERSHEY'S Cocoa**
- 2 **teaspoons powdered instant coffee**
- 1 **teaspoon vanilla extract**

Beat cream, powdered sugar, cocoa, instant coffee and vanilla in small mixer bowl until cream starts to thicken, but is still pourable. Do not overbeat.

Holiday Double Peanut Butter Fudge Cookies

1 can (14 ounces) sweetened condensed milk (not evaporated milk)

³/₄ cup REESE'S Creamy Peanut Butter

2 cups all-purpose biscuit baking mix

1 teaspoon vanilla extract

³/₄ cup REESE'S Peanut Butter Chips

¹/₄ cup granulated sugar

¹/₂ teaspoon red colored sugar

¹/₂ teaspoon green colored sugar

1. Heat oven to 375°F.

2. Beat sweetened condensed milk and peanut butter in large bowl with electric mixer on medium speed until smooth. Beat in baking mix and vanilla; stir in peanut butter chips. Set aside.

3. Stir together granulated sugar and colored sugars in small bowl. Shape dough into 1-inch balls; roll in sugar. Place 2 inches apart on ungreased cookie sheet; flatten slightly with bottom of glass.

4. Bake 6 to 8 minutes or until very lightly browned (do not overbake). Cool slightly. Remove to wire rack and cool completely. Store in tightly covered container.

Chocolate and Orange Meltaways

Makes 2 dozen pieces

2 cups (12-ounce package) HERSHEY'S Premier White Chips, divided

$1/2$ cup (1 stick) unsalted butter (do not substitute margarine)

$1/3$ cup whipping cream

$1^1/_2$ teaspoons orange extract

CHOCOLATE COATING (recipe follows)

$1/2$ teaspoon shortening (do not use butter, margarine, spread or oil)

1. Line tray with wax paper. Reserve 2 tablespoons white chips.

2. Combine butter and whipping cream in medium saucepan; cook over low heat, stirring constantly until mixture comes to a full rolling boil. Remove from heat; immediately add remaining white chips. Stir with whisk until smooth. Add orange extract; blend well.

3. Refrigerate until firm enough to handle, about 2 hours. Taking small amount of mixture at a time, shape into 1-inch balls. Place on prepared tray; refrigerate until firm, about $1^1/_2$ hours. Prepare CHOCOLATE COATING. Place one candy onto fork; dip into coating, covering completely and allowing excess to drip off. Place candies onto prepared tray. Repeat with remaining candies. Refrigerate until coating is set, about 1 hour.

4. Place reserved 2 tablespoons white chips and shortening in small microwave-safe bowl. Microwave at MEDIUM (50%) 30 seconds; stir. If necessary, microwave at MEDIUM an additional 10 seconds or until mixture is smooth when stirred. With fork, lightly drizzle over coated candies; refrigerate until set, about 20 minutes. Cover; store in refrigerator.

Chocolate Coating: Place 2 packages (4 ounces each) HERSHEY'S Semi-Sweet Chocolate Baking Bars, broken into pieces, and 1 teaspoon shortening (do not use butter, margarine, spread or oil) in medium microwave-safe bowl. Microwave at MEDIUM (50%) 2 minutes; stir. If necessary, microwave at MEDIUM an additional 15 seconds at a time, stirring after each heating, until chocolate is melted and mixture is smooth when stirred. Cool slightly. (If chocolate is too hot, it will not coat candy.)

Chocolate Cake Squares with Eggnog Sauce

Makes 12 to 15 servings

1¹/₂ teaspoons baking soda

1 cup buttermilk or sour milk*

³/₄ cup HERSHEY'S Cocoa

³/₄ cup boiling water

¹/₄ cup (¹/₂ stick) butter or margarine, softened

¹/₄ cup shortening

2 cups sugar

2 eggs

1 teaspoon vanilla extract

¹/₈ teaspoon salt

1³/₄ cups all-purpose flour

EGGNOG SAUCE (recipe follows)

To sour milk: Use 1 tablespoon white vinegar plus milk to equal 1 cup.

1. Heat oven to 350°F. Grease and flour 13×9×2-inch baking pan.

2. Stir baking soda into buttermilk in medium bowl; set aside. Stir together cocoa and water until smooth; set aside.

3. Beat butter, shortening and sugar in large bowl until creamy. Add eggs, vanilla and salt; beat well. Add buttermilk mixture alternately with flour to butter mixture, beating until blended. Add cocoa mixture; blend thoroughly. Pour batter into prepared pan.

4. Bake 40 to 45 minutes or until wooden pick inserted in center comes out clean. Cool completely. Serve with EGGNOG SAUCE.

Eggnog Sauce

1 tablespoon cornstarch

2 tablespoons cold water

1¹/₃ cups milk

¹/₄ cup sugar

3 egg yolks, beaten

¹/₄ teaspoon each brandy and vanilla extracts

Several dashes ground nutmeg

Stir cornstarch and water in saucepan until smooth. Add milk, sugar and egg yolks. Beat with whisk until well blended. Cook over medium heat, stirring constantly, until thickened. Remove from heat. Stir in extracts. Cool completely. Sprinkle nutmeg over top. Cover; refrigerate leftover sauce.

Makes about 1³/₄ cups sauce

Holiday Red Raspberry Chocolate Bars

Makes 24 to 36 bars

2½ cups all-purpose flour

1 cup sugar

¾ cup finely chopped pecans

1 egg, beaten

1 cup (2 sticks) cold butter or margarine

1 jar (12 ounces) seedless red raspberry jam

1⅔ cups HERSHEY'S Milk Chocolate Chips, HERSHEY'S SPECIAL DARK Chocolate Chips, HERSHEY'S Semi-Sweet Chocolate Chips or HERSHEY'S MINI KISSESBRAND Milk Chocolates

1. Heat oven to 350°F. Grease 13×9×2-inch baking pan.

2. Stir together flour, sugar, pecans and egg in large bowl. Cut in butter with pastry blender or fork until mixture resembles coarse crumbs; set aside 1½ cups crumb mixture. Press remaining crumb mixture on bottom of prepared pan. Stir jam to soften; carefully spread over crumb mixture in pan. Sprinkle with chocolate chips. Crumble reserved crumb mixture evenly over top.

3. Bake 40 to 45 minutes or until lightly browned. Cool completely in pan on wire rack; cut into bars.

Peanut Butter Holiday Cheesecake

Makes 12 to 14 servings

6 tablespoons butter or margarine, melted

6 tablespoons HERSHEY'S Cocoa

$^1/_3$ cup powdered sugar

$1^1/_2$ cups vanilla wafer cookie crumbs (about 45 cookies, crushed)

1 package (8 ounces) cream cheese, softened

2 tablespoons lemon juice

$1^1/_2$ cups REESE'S Peanut Butter Chips

1 can (14 ounces) sweetened condensed milk (not evaporated milk)

1 cup ($^1/_2$ pint) whipping cream, whipped

CRANBERRY TOPPING (recipe follows)

1. Stir together butter, cocoa, powdered sugar and vanilla wafer crumbs in bowl. Press firmly onto bottom of 9-inch springform pan; refrigerate while preparing filling.

2. Beat cream cheese and lemon juice in large bowl until fluffy; set aside. Combine peanut butter chips and sweetened condensed milk in medium saucepan over low heat; stir constantly until chips are melted and mixture is smooth. Add to cream cheese mixture; blend well. Fold in whipped cream. Pour evenly over crumb crust.

3. Cover; refrigerate while preparing CRANBERRY TOPPING. Spread topping evenly over cheesecake. Cover; refrigerate several hours or overnight. Remove side of springform pan to serve. Cover; refrigerate leftover cheesecake.

Cranberry Topping

**2 cups fresh or frozen
    cranberries**

1 cup sugar

³/₄ cup water, divided

2 tablespoons cornstarch

1 teaspoon vanilla extract

1. Stir together cranberries, sugar and ¹/₂ cup water in medium saucepan. Cook over medium heat, stirring occasionally, until mixture comes to a boil. Reduce heat; simmer 3 minutes. Remove from heat.

2. Stir together cornstarch and remaining ¹/₄ cup water; gradually add to cranberry mixture. Return to heat; stir constantly until mixture thickens and resembles fruit preserves (about 4 minutes). Cool to room temperature; stir in vanilla.

Makes about 3¹/₂ cups topping

MINI KISSES® Pumpkin Mousse Cups

1³/₄ **cups (10-ounce package) HERSHEY'S MINI KISSES**BRAND **Milk Chocolates, divided**

24 **large marshmallows**

¹/₂ **cup milk**

¹/₂ **cup canned pumpkin**

1 **teaspoon vanilla extract**

1 **teaspoon pumpkin pie spice**

¹/₃ **cup powdered sugar**

1 **cup (¹/₂ pint) cold whipping cream**

Additional sweetened whipped cream (optional)

1. Line 10 muffin cups (2¹/₂ inches in diameter) with paper bake cups. Reserve ¹/₂ cup chocolate pieces. Place remaining 1¹/₄ cups chocolates in small microwave-safe bowl; microwave at MEDIUM (50%) 1 minute or until melted when stirred. Mixture should be thick.

2. Very thickly coat inside pleated surfaces and bottoms of bake cups with melted chocolate using soft pastry brush. Refrigerate 10 minutes; recoat any thin spots with melted chocolate.* Refrigerate until firm, about 2 hours. Gently peel off paper; refrigerate until ready to fill.

3. Place marshmallows, milk and pumpkin in medium microwave-safe bowl. Microwave at MEDIUM 1 minute; stir. Microwave additional 30 seconds at a time, stirring after each heating, until mixture is melted and smooth. Stir in vanilla and pumpkin pie spice. Cool completely.

4. Beat powdered sugar and whipping cream until stiff; fold into pumpkin mixture. Fill cups with pumpkin mousse; garnish with reserved chocolate pieces and sweetened whipped cream, if desired. Cover; refrigerate 2 hours or until firm.

If reheating is needed, microwave chocolate at MEDIUM 15 seconds; stir.

Holiday Fudge Torte

Makes 8 to 10 servings

1 **cup all-purpose flour**

³/₄ **cup sugar**

¹/₄ **cup HERSHEY'S Cocoa**

1¹/₂ **teaspoons powdered instant coffee**

³/₄ **teaspoon baking soda**

¹/₄ **teaspoon salt**

¹/₂ **cup (1 stick) butter or margarine, softened**

³/₄ **cup dairy sour cream**

1 **egg**

¹/₂ **teaspoon vanilla extract**
   FUDGE NUT GLAZE (recipe follows)

1. Heat oven to 350°F. Grease 9-inch round baking pan; line bottom with wax paper. Grease paper; flour paper and pan.

2. Stir together flour, sugar, cocoa, instant coffee, baking soda and salt in large bowl. Add butter, sour cream, egg and vanilla; beat on low speed of mixer until blended. Increase speed to medium; beat 3 minutes. Pour batter into prepared pan.

3. Bake 30 to 35 minutes or until wooden pick inserted in center comes out clean. Cool 10 minutes. Remove from pan to wire rack; gently peel off wax paper. Cool completely.

4. Prepare FUDGE NUT GLAZE.

5. Place cake on serving plate; pour glaze evenly over cake, allowing some to run down sides. Refrigerate until glaze is firm, about 1 hour. Cover; refrigerate leftover torte.

Fudge Nut Glaze

¹/₂ **cup whipping cream**

¹/₄ **cup sugar**

1 **tablespoon butter**

1¹/₂ **teaspoons light corn syrup**

¹/₃ **cup HERSHEY'S SPECIAL DARK Chocolate Chips or HERSHEY'S Semi-Sweet Chocolate Chips**

³/₄ **cup chopped MAUNA LOA Macadamia Nuts, hazelnuts or pecans**

¹/₂ **teaspoon vanilla extract**

1. Combine all ingredients except nuts and vanilla in small saucepan. Cook over medium heat, stirring constantly, until mixture boils. Cook, stirring constantly, 5 minutes. Remove from heat.

2. Cool 10 minutes; stir in nuts and vanilla.

Irish Chocolate Mint Dessert

1¹/₂ cups (3 sticks) plus
  6 tablespoons butter or
  margarine, divided

2 cups granulated sugar

2 teaspoons vanilla extract

4 eggs

1 cup all-purpose flour

³/₄ cup HERSHEY'S Cocoa

¹/₂ teaspoon baking powder

2²/₃ cups powdered sugar

1 tablespoon plus 1 teaspoon
  water

1 teaspoon mint extract

4 drops green food color

1 cup HERSHEY'S SPECIAL
  DARK Chocolate Chips or
  HERSHEY'S Semi-Sweet
  Chocolate Chips

1. Heat oven to 350°F. Grease 13×9×2-inch baking pan.

2. Place 1 cup (2 sticks) butter in large microwave-safe bowl; cover. Microwave at MEDIUM (50%) 2 minutes or until melted. Stir in granulated sugar and vanilla. Add eggs; beat well. Add flour, cocoa and baking powder; beat until well blended. Pour batter into prepared pan.

3. Bake 30 to 35 minutes or until wooden pick inserted in center comes out clean. Cool completely in pan on wire rack.

4. Prepare mint cream center by combining powdered sugar, ¹/₂ cup (1 stick) butter, water, mint extract and food color in large bowl. Beat until smooth. Spread evenly on brownies. Cover; refrigerate until cold.

5. Prepare chocolate glaze by placing remaining 6 tablespoons butter and chocolate chips in small microwave-safe bowl. Microwave at MEDIUM 1 minute or until mixture is smooth when stirred. Cool slightly; pour over chilled dessert. Cover; refrigerate at least 1 hour before serving. Cover; refrigerate leftover dessert.

Pinecone Cookies

6 tablespoons butter or margarine

$^1/_3$ cup HERSHEY'S Cocoa or HERSHEY'S SPECIAL DARK Cocoa

1 cup sugar

2 eggs

1 teaspoon vanilla extract

2 cups all-purpose flour

$^1/_2$ teaspoon baking powder

$^1/_2$ teaspoon salt

$^1/_4$ teaspoon baking soda

Light corn syrup

Sliced almonds

1. Melt butter in small saucepan; remove from heat. Add cocoa; blend well. Beat sugar, eggs and vanilla in large bowl; blend in cocoa mixture. Stir together flour, baking powder, salt and baking soda; add to cocoa mixture, beating until smooth. Refrigerate dough about 1 hour or until firm enough to roll.

2. Heat oven to 350°F. Lightly grease cookie sheet or line with parchment paper. Roll small portion of dough between two pieces of wax paper to $^1/_8$-inch thickness. Cut into pinecone shapes using 2- or 2$^1/_2$-inch oval cookie cutter. Place on prepared cookie sheet; lightly brush cookies with corn syrup. Arrange almonds in pinecone fashion; lightly drizzle or brush almonds with corn syrup. Repeat with remaining dough.

3. Bake 7 to 8 minutes or until set. Remove from cookie sheet to wire rack; cool completely.

Red Velvet Cake Roll

1/4 cup powdered sugar

4 eggs, separated

1/2 cup plus 1/3 cup granulated sugar, divided

1 teaspoon vanilla extract

2 tablespoons (1-ounce bottle) red food color

Water

2/3 cup all-purpose flour

1/4 cup HERSHEY'S Cocoa

1/2 teaspoon baking powder

1/4 teaspoon baking soda

1/8 teaspoon salt

CREAM CHEESE FILLING (recipe follows)

Additional powdered sugar

HERSHEY'S Syrup

1. Heat oven to 375°F. Line 15½×10½×1-inch jelly-roll pan with foil; generously grease foil. Sprinkle linen or clean towel with ¼ cup powdered sugar

2. Beat egg whites in large bowl until soft peaks form; gradually add ½ cup granulated sugar, beating until stiff peaks form. Beat egg yolks and vanilla in medium bowl on medium speed of mixer 3 minutes. Gradually add remaining ⅓ cup granulated sugar; continue beating 2 additional minutes.

3. Place red food color in liquid measuring cup; add water to make ⅓ cup. Stir together flour, cocoa, baking powder, baking soda and salt. Add to egg yolk mixture alternately with colored water, beating on low speed just until batter is smooth. Gradually fold chocolate mixture into beaten egg whites until well blended. Spread batter evenly in prepared pan.

4. Bake 12 to 15 minutes or until top springs back when touched lightly in center. Immediately loosen cake from edges of pan; invert onto prepared towel. Carefully peel off foil. Immediately roll cake and towel together starting from narrow end; place on wire rack to cool completely.

5. Prepare CREAM CHEESE FILLING. Carefully unroll cake; remove towel. Spread filling over cake. Reroll cake without towel. Wrap filled cake with wax paper and wrap again with plastic wrap. Refrigerate with seam down at least 1 hour or until ready to serve. Just before serving, sprinkle top with additional powdered sugar. Serve drizzled with syrup and garnished as desired. Cover; refrigerate leftover cake roll.

Cream Cheese Filling: Beat
1 package (8 ounces) softened
cream cheese, 1 cup powdered
sugar, 6 tablespoons softened butter
or margarine and 1 teaspoon vanilla
extract in small mixer bowl until
smooth.

C

Cakes

Candy

Index

METRIC CONVERSION CHART

VOLUME MEASUREMENTS (dry)

$\frac{1}{8}$ teaspoon = 0.5 mL
$\frac{1}{4}$ teaspoon = 1 mL
$\frac{1}{2}$ teaspoon = 2 mL
$\frac{3}{4}$ teaspoon = 4 mL
1 teaspoon = 5 mL
1 tablespoon = 15 mL
2 tablespoons = 30 mL
$\frac{1}{4}$ cup = 60 mL
$\frac{1}{3}$ cup = 75 mL
$\frac{1}{2}$ cup = 125 mL
$\frac{2}{3}$ cup = 150 mL
$\frac{3}{4}$ cup = 175 mL
1 cup = 250 mL
2 cups = 1 pint = 500 mL
3 cups = 750 mL
4 cups = 1 quart = 1 L

VOLUME MEASUREMENTS (fluid)

1 fluid ounce (2 tablespoons) = 30 mL
4 fluid ounces ($\frac{1}{2}$ cup) = 125 mL
8 fluid ounces (1 cup) = 250 mL
12 fluid ounces (1$\frac{1}{2}$ cups) = 375 mL
16 fluid ounces (2 cups) = 500 mL

WEIGHTS (mass)

$\frac{1}{2}$ ounce = 15 g
1 ounce = 30 g
3 ounces = 90 g
4 ounces = 120 g
8 ounces = 225 g
10 ounces = 285 g
12 ounces = 360 g
16 ounces = 1 pound = 450 g

DIMENSIONS

$\frac{1}{16}$ inch = 2 mm
$\frac{1}{8}$ inch = 3 mm
$\frac{1}{4}$ inch = 6 mm
$\frac{1}{2}$ inch = 1.5 cm
$\frac{3}{4}$ inch = 2 cm
1 inch = 2.5 cm

OVEN TEMPERATURES

250°F = 120°C
275°F = 140°C
300°F = 150°C
325°F = 160°C
350°F = 180°C
375°F = 190°C
400°F = 200°C
425°F = 220°C
450°F = 230°C

BAKING PAN SIZES

Utensil	Size in Inches/Quarts	Metric Volume	Size in Centimeters
Baking or Cake Pan (square or rectangular)	8×8×2	2 L	20×20×5
	9×9×2	2.5 L	23×23×5
	12×8×2	3 L	30×20×5
	13×9×2	3.5 L	33×23×5
Loaf Pan	8×4×3	1.5 L	20×10×7
	9×5×3	2 L	23×13×7
Round Layer Cake Pan	8×1½	1.2 L	20×4
	9×1½	1.5 L	23×4
Pie Plate	8×1¼	750 mL	20×3
	9×1¼	1 L	23×3
Baking Dish or Casserole	1 quart	1 L	—
	1½ quarts	1.5 L	—
	2 quarts	2 L	—